NARCISSISTIC MOTHERS

The Complete Guide for Daughters with CPTSD of Immature, Emotionally Absent Mothers with Borderline Behaviors

HAPPINESS FACTORY
Be Who you Want!

Text Copyright © Happiness Factory

All rights reserved. No part of this guide may be reproduced in any form without permission in writing from the publisher except in the case of brief quotations embodied in critical articles or reviews.

Legal & Disclaimer

The information contained in this book and its contents is not designed to replace or take the place of any form of medical or professional advice and is not meant to replace the need for independent medical, financial, legal, or other professional advice or services, as may be required. The content and information in this book have been provided for educational and entertainment purposes only.

The content and information contained in this book have been compiled from sources deemed reliable, and it is accurate to the best of the Author's knowledge, information, and belief. However, the Author cannot guarantee its accuracy and validity and cannot be held liable for any errors and/or omissions. Further, changes are periodically made to this book as and when needed. Where appropriate and/or necessary, you must consult a professional (including but not limited to your doctor, attorney, financial advisor, or such other professional advisor) before using any of the suggested remedies, techniques, or information in this book.

Upon using the contents and information contained in this book, you agree to hold harmless the Author from and against any damages, costs, and expenses, including any legal fees potentially resulting from the application of any of the information provided by this book. This disclaimer applies to any loss, damages, or injury caused by the use and application, whether directly or indirectly, of any advice or information presented, whether for breach of contract, tort, negligence, personal injury, criminal intent, or under any other cause of action.

You agree to accept all risks of using the information presented inside this book.

You agree that by continuing to read this book, where appropriate and/or necessary, you shall consult a professional (including but not limited to your doctor, attorney, or financial advisor, or such other advisor as needed) before using any of the suggested remedies, techniques, or information in this book.

ABOUT HAPPINESS FACTORY

BRING HAPPINESS INTO YOUR LIFE

Do you feel as though your life lacks love and happiness?

Do you want to beat your anxiety and depression and live your life to the fullest?

Do you feel undervalued in your professional life?

Do you want to make positive changes in your behavior?

You may be surprised to discover that, every day, countless people are having these same thoughts and feelings. We understand how challenging life's problems can be, and we want to help guide you through them.

At Happiness Factory, we devise content for men and women to identify, understand, and sort through their problems, ultimately bringing happiness to their lives. With some alteration to your mindset and how you process emotions, many of life's issues can be resolved. We'll help bring peace and stability to your professional and personal life.

Experiencing happiness can fundamentally change how we think, act, and live our lives. Negative experiences can minimize or eliminate joy from our life, and this is why our researchers provide insight into the best possible solutions to your problems. Our goal is to ensure that you're happy, healthy, and confident so you can tackle anything that comes your way.

By reading our books, you'll be able to understand what goes on in your mind. You'll discover how your body reacts to the different types of mental and emotional stress you face in your personal and professional life. From problems in your relationships to work-related stress, we at Happiness Factory will help you channel your inner strength to conquer any problem in any sphere of your life.

Learn how to live your best life with the help of the Happiness Factory Book Collection.

TABLE OF CONTENTS

- INTRODUCTION 1
  - Overview: Healing From Narcissistic Abuse 3
- Chapter 1 - WHAT IS NARCISSISTIC PERSONALITY DISORDER? 10
- Chapter 2 - WHAT IS A NARCISSISTIC MOTHER? 13
- Chapter 3 - DETAILED CHARACTERISTICS OF A NARCISSIST . 16
- Chapter 4 - TYPES OF NARCISSISM 21
- Chapter 5 - DIAGNOSING NARCISSISM 31
- Chapter 6 - THE NARCISSISTIC MOTHER-DAUGHTER RELATIONSHIP 33
  - Childhood Emotional Narcissistic Abuse 39
- Chapter 7 - ADULT DAUGHTERS OF NARCISSISTIC MOTHERS: AN OVERVIEW 51
- Chapter 8 - THE EFFECTS OF NARCISSISTIC PARENTING 54
  - Effects of Narcissistic Abuse: Beyond Childhood 59
- Chapter 9 - THE ABUSIVE NARCISSISTIC MOTHER: SYMPTOMS, CAUSES, AND HOW TO RECOVER 64
  - Symptoms of Narcissistic Mother Syndrome 64
  - Causes of Narcissistic Mother Syndrome 67
  - Recovering From Narcissistic Abuse 68

Chapter 10 - MENTAL MANIPULATION AND CONTROL BY NARCISSISTIC MOTHERS 74

Chapter 11 - NARCISSISTIC STRATEGIES OF MANIPULATION . 80

Chapter 12 - NARCISSISTS AND THEIR LIES 92

Chapter 13 - THE THREE STAGES OF HEALING FROM NARCISSISTIC ABUSE 98

Chapter 14 - A NARCISSISTIC MOTHER: FALSE SELF AND ENMESHMENT 101

Chapter 15 - SEPARATION FROM A NARCISSISTIC MOTHER: THE PATH TO HEALING AND RECOVERY 105

Chapter 16 - RESETTING YOUR MINDSET: BEYOND TOXIC PARENTING 113

Chapter 17 - THE ART OF MEDITATION 126

Chapter 18 - HOW TO START HEALING FROM NARCISSISTIC PARENTING 133

Chapter 19 - HOW TO HEAL FROM COMPLEX POST-TRAUMATIC STRESS DISORDER (CPTSD) CAUSED BY A NARCISSISTIC PARENT 139

    Healing From Emotional Flashbacks 141

    Healing From Toxic Shame 142

    Healing From Self-Abandonment 145

    Healing From Your Inner Critic 147

Chapter 20 - STOP LABELING YOURSELF AS A VICTIM: SEVEN
WAYS TO HEAL... 150

CONCLUSION 156

THANK YOU 157

INTRODUCTION

ARE YOU THE CHILD OF A MOTHER with a narcissistic personality disorder (NPD)? If yes, you may find it hard to trust people or have meaningful relationships. It's likely that your self-esteem, self-worth, and sense of identity have suffered as a consequence of narcissistic parenting.

This book will help you discover what exactly narcissistic parenting is. It's a detailed, in-depth analysis of narcissistic mothers (NMs), describing how this type of parent thinks and feels about herself, her child, and those outside of her family. It explains what it's like to be the child of an NM. Here, we illuminate the path for the NM's adult-child, guiding you through the process towards healing.

One could argue that there's a special place in Hell reserved for the type of mother who tries to feel superior by manipulating her children. These are the harmful actions and behavior of a narcissist. WebMD defines narcissism as "extreme self-involvement to the degree that it makes a person ignore the needs of those around them."[1] An NM lacks empathy, disregards her child's feelings,

---

[1] WebMD contributors, "Narcissism: Symptoms and Signs" *WebMD*, https://www.webmd.com/mental-health/narcissism-symptoms-signs

depriving the child of their basic needs. As a result, the child often expresses anger, depression, anxiety, low self-esteem, and sadness.

If you notice this mothering pattern within yourself, you need to take a step back and make some profound changes. As well as this book, reading other experts' work on the subject will help you realize that the woman you're becoming is emotionally and psychologically abusive.

We'll unravel the mystery of narcissism, giving information on NMs and toxic parents, helping you understand how you may have been psychologically manipulated as a child. We'll teach you how to heal, reclaim your power, and learn to love and accept yourself again after years of narcissistic abuse and trauma at the hands of a narcissistic parent.

This book isn't just for narcissistic parents hoping to make a change — it's for the children of these narcissists too. As the adult child of a narcissist, it'll give you a deeper understanding of what traits your narcissistic parent showed and how these impacted you. This understanding will help heal the overwhelming emotional pain caused by being raised by an NM.

The book includes insight into manipulation and emotional freezing — some types of abuse inflicted on children by NMs. We'll present various coping skills within our recovery program for NMs, narcissists, and their families.

This book is based on reality. You'll discover the truth behind narcissistic parenting through the contributions of real-life people with real-life stories to share. We hope that it'll help you recover from past trauma and prepare you for a life of happiness, fulfillment, and satisfying relationships.

OVERVIEW: HEALING FROM NARCISSISTIC ABUSE

Embarking on the path of recovery from narcissistic abuse is a challenging one. It's a journey that needs to be taken with strength, courage, and determination. Many victims have a difficult time moving on from toxic and abusive relationships. They allow their past and their negative childhood experiences to cling to their hearts and minds.

It doesn't have to be this way. Healing from emotional abuse in childhood can be accomplished safely and healthily. To heal from the effects of narcissistic abuse, the victim needs to think of themselves as a fighter. They have to recover from their childhood's mental scars, stop blaming themselves for their past experiences, and rise above the toxic energy poisoning their lives.

It *is* possible. You can get there. For each and every victim of childhood abuse, happiness and healing are within their reach.

How much do you know about NMs? What does the word "narcissism" mean to you? Did you grow up with an NM? How has being involved with a narcissist personally affected you? The most important part of facing past abuse is to know why it happened and what role you played in it. You need to understand that you didn't deserve it and that it wasn't your fault.

Life with a narcissist is measured out by narcissistic abuse and trauma. In most cases, children raised by narcissists are brought up in an environment of emotional incest and emotional freezing. The trauma this inflicts can cause childhood wounds that never heal. To heal means accepting that trauma through working on one's adult self and moving towards wholeness.

This book unravels the mystery of your past, helps you understand the subject of narcissism, and gives you tools to heal and recover from an NM.

You'll learn what or who an NM is. You'll begin to identify the narcissism inflicted on you by your parent and to recognize the emotional and psychological abuse you suffered. You'll start to become aware of the lack of trust, love, and emotional bonds you experienced, as well as the absence of feeling seen or heard.

It'll become clear how you came to feel so broken inside and how you exhibit signs and symptoms of trauma.

Once you're able to get past the shame and work through the trauma, you'll be able to start living a happy and fulfilling life.

This book is divided into sections where you can read one topic at a time. Allow yourself to absorb what you've learned before moving on to the next. It may be a difficult read. Many readers find it hard to get through specific chapters without them triggering stressful or painful memories. But we urge you to persevere. By getting through the book in its entirety, you'll find that the knowledge you gain will provide relief from the weight of your past trauma and pain.

There are many narcissists out there. Perhaps you know one personally. You could even be the child of one. If you had an NM, she was incapable of loving you unconditionally or seeing you as an independent being. Her possessive and manipulative behavior would have been running themes throughout all the relationships in her life.

But you don't have to let your past define you. You can have a sane, pain-free, and joyful life in which you don't repeat the patterns of your past. You can live a life of contentment, pleasure, gratitude, and love. It's never too early or too late to begin your healing journey. As you start to heal, you'll begin to let go of the pain. All the fears that have built up over time will fade, and you'll be able to face your future with fresh hope. Soon, you'll be able to live your life with no fear at all.

We dedicate this book to the many women who carry the unwarranted burden of betrayal and abuse by an NM. We know the pain and hurt inflicted by such parents and stand with these brave survivors.

* * *

Here's a story from one of our contributors:

My journey to contributing to this book started as a child. I had two role models who were narcissists: my mother and maternal grandfather. They didn't care about anyone but themselves. I realized early on that my mother was determined to hurt me, devalue me, and make me feel inadequate. But she would never admit it to the cruelty she inflicted on me. She would never admit that she was at fault. She never allowed me to see her as a deeply disturbed woman who was also suffering from her abusive childhood. She never let me feel any empathy for her. She managed to convince me that I was the one that was wrong instead of looking at herself and seeing a very unstable woman. It's the same reason why she refused to see that her father was troubled too.

It's seriously wrong when parents make their children feel inadequate and uncomfortable. The children of narcissists will continually feel insecure around their parents, but for no obvious reason. When you sit down with a narcissist, it's like you disappear. You become invisible to them. They don't listen to you. They act like the only thing that matters is themselves. This behavior is why we learn to dissociate ourselves from them. We emotionally freeze and detach from them to survive.

Often, years later, when a narcissistic parent comes back into your life, they manage to pull you out of your place of healing. This happened to me, and it's a significant problem for children of narcissists. You start to rebuild your world and pull yourself out of the pain, and then suddenly, you're back to how you felt when you were four years old. It's like you're watching TV, and they suddenly appear on the screen. You start to re-live the abuse all over again.

All of this affects your other relationships too. Just as you start to get into your safety zone, you suddenly find yourself in the pain of childhood again. The narcissist and the psychopath are like *predatory shadows. They'll always find a way to get your attention. That's why you have to detach yourself from them; to dissociate. You have to learn to trust your gut instinct and tell yourself that no one else's input matters but yours.*

You need to dig deep and see if any specific situations or triggers take you back to your childhood trauma so that you can face them head-on. You'll learn to listen to the little voice inside of you. You'll notice that you're not as emotionally connected to the narcissist as you used to be. As you mature emotionally, you'll be able to be around them without dissociating or freezing. You'll see that it's not the narcissist who's influencing you and your feelings. It's your attachment to them, your fear of being ashamed or embarrassed, and your sense of being a victim that holds you back. These thoughts are typical for adults who've been emotionally abused as children and are now in relationships.

When you're emotionally attached to someone, it gives them power over you. You allow yourself to be manipulated and controlled to a certain extent. But with narcissists, this is amplified and affects your relationships throughout your life. Your fears of being ashamed or embarrassed make you feel uncomfortable and humiliated. You need to remember: you're not the victim of the narcissist. You're the one mistreating yourself by allowing yourself to be manipulated and controlled, even years after leaving them. No one can tell you what to do with your own life. I know from personal experience what it's like to face this, even years after the abuse. But you can get past it. It'll take time and requires pain, dedication, and patience. You'll need to understand that you suffered much damage to get this way.

That's why it'll take work to get out of it. But you can do it. Just take the courage to move to the other side of your fears.

There's a lot more that I could say about this, but I'll leave it at this for now:

I could write hundreds of books on this subject. It's been my life's work. All of my books are fiction, but they come from a place that's real to me. This information is here to help any woman understand her early life experiences as a young girl. I'm sure you can understand why a woman would be attracted to a seemingly charming psychopath or a narcissist. It would be a certain happiness compared to a childhood with an abusive mother. But hopefully, my words will help them realize that they risk falling into yet a new life of misery and that they should run a mile from these happiness-vampires.

The thing that's been essential in my journey to healing, which I can pass on to other women, is remembering that you're an individual in your own right. You may come from an abusive background, but you're important, and you have a voice. You're valuable enough to be worth saving. You deserve time, patience, education, and self-worth.

My goal is to get all the information out there in the hopes that it'll help someone. The biggest problem is that we, as a society, don't want to listen to female advice. It's not considered a viable option. Women seem to be seen as the lesser sex all the time. I was in a relationship with a man who'd tell me that I was too sensitive or too emotional. Women are generally labeled like this, and I started to wonder if it were true. But it's not. We're individuals, and the fact is that we are who we are. We can either try to improve ourselves or accept ourselves.

I chose to improve myself. I know what it is to go to therapy. I know what it is to have friends who want to help me. Now, I'm content and happy that I'm alive and have removed myself from my abusers. I know what it is to do new things. I have a good time with my friends and close family members. We laugh and enjoy each other's company. I work and have a great life. I get to say what I want to my mother and other people in my life. I don't need anyone's permission to be who I am.

Sometimes when I want to discuss things that I've learned from my various relationships, I'm told to keep quiet. But I want to share with people my experience in the hope that it can help them face their past and better their future.

By reading on, you'll be taking the first steps towards your new life. You'll start to walk away from the pain and madness caused by narcissistic parenting. Nothing you've experienced so far has been a waste of time. You can use it to push yourself forward and into a happier existence.

Don't let this opportunity pass you by. Don't start to read this book and stop because it's too painful. It's a gift that'll help you create a whole new life. There's nothing to fear. This book will give you strength, hope, and a foundation for a fresh start. Be free to live your life—how *you* want to live it.

CHAPTER 1

WHAT IS NARCISSISTIC PERSONALITY DISORDER?

A NARCISSISTIC PERSONALITY DISORDER (NPD) is a pervasive and enduring pattern of inner experiences and behaviors that harms an individual's mental health and interpersonal relationships. This condition affects an estimated 1% of the general population in the United States or about 6,742,000 adults.

An exaggerated sense of self-importance and a lack of empathy characterizes NPD, with a deep need for recognition and admiration from others. All of these traits serve to construct and maintain a grandiose self-view. Those with the condition are more likely to suffer from eating disorders, hypochondria, and other phobias.

Narcissistic individuals often have a history of being teased or criticized by others which may explain their need to feel superior and unique. They're often exploitive of others, using them to boost their fragile sense of self.

Narcissists possess a deep need for attention, admiration, acceptance, affirmation, and reinforcement. They have a sense of entitlement and a particular belief that they're better than others.

People with NPD behave arrogantly and selfishly. They're prone to having affairs and sexual relationships with multiple partners. They're more likely to engage in masochistic or sadomasochistic acts and exhibitionism. They may display improper behavior and show off their physical appearance in inappropriate ways.

Narcissists frequently exhibit jealous tendencies, viewing others as potential rivals. They may seek other people's weaknesses to obtain admiration for themselves. Despite outward appearances, they have a sense of inferiority and can anger quickly. They're prone to showing intense negative reactions to disappointing events and experience frequent mood swings, such as elation, depression, and suicidal thoughts. Because of this, they face difficulties in establishing and maintaining stable relationships.

A narcissist essentially feels empty inside and devoid of all meaning. To fill this void, they may choose wealth and power as the center of their life. They may spend copious amounts of money and feel a sense of urgency in everything they do. Theirs is a superficial world based on outward appearances and the need to excel at all costs.

Complex Post-Traumatic Stress Disorder (CPTSD)

Complex post-traumatic stress disorder (CPTSD) refers to chronic psychological and physiological stress resulting from prolonged trauma, which can develop into a personality disorder. It's said to be a more severe and long-lasting version of post-traumatic stress disorder (PTSD). The development of CPTSD is associated with the traumatic experience of people subjected to recurring episodes of psychological trauma that are interpersonal, methodical, and intentional.

Developmental Trauma Disorder (DTD)

Developmental trauma disorder (DTD) is a psychiatric, developmental disorder associated with a history of chronic interpersonal abuse, neglect, or exposure to extreme traumatic stress. Like other types of trauma survivors, individuals diagnosed with DTD experience flashbacks, nightmares, and intrusive thoughts that can be debilitating to the point of interfering with personal relationships and their everyday functioning. However, unlike patients with PTSD, patients with DTD don't have the characteristic avoidance of trauma reminders. They tend to have a greater dissociation level from their symptoms.

Emotional Abuse

Emotional abuse is a form of mental cruelty that can include rejection, constant criticism, manipulation, humiliation, intimidation, and/or other forms of verbal or emotional trauma.

CHAPTER 2

WHAT IS A NARCISSISTIC MOTHER?

THE NM IS A MOTHER who displays the classic symptoms of NPD—she puts herself first and can't relate to her children securely or reasonably. She brings negative feelings and emotions into the household, making those around her feel uncomfortable and worthless. An NM will coerce you into being on her side despite her actions and behavior. Unfortunately, it's not uncommon for children to be brought up by an NM. The effects of the emotional abuse it causes can be long-lasting.

An abuser can have a dual personality: one side is nice, and the other is manipulative and aggressive. This can make growing up with one confusing and disorientating. When you're a child, your NM can act like a "normal" parent while subtly making you feel bad about yourself and the things you like. She'll try to control who you are as a person. As a teenager, she may force you to depend on her and strip you of your independence. When you become an adult, your NM may try to harm you physically if she doesn't get her way.

The NM is a particular type of parent who works hard to convince her children that she's the one who defines what it is to be a worthwhile person in this world. The relationship with her child isn't a healthy one. She has a deep need for her child's attention, love, and approval, but she doesn't know how to express it herself. She uses her child for self-validation, neglecting her duty to nurture and love unconditionally.

A "normal" mother says to her child, "I love you. I'm proud of you and what you do. I'm your greatest cheerleader." Instead, an NM looks at her child and thinks, "I want you to look at me and idolize me. I want you to think I'm the most wonderful person in the world. I won't say this to you—you should just know it. I shouldn't have to ask you for adoration; you should just give it."

An NM is haughty and filled with a false sense of self as she papers over the cracks of her fragile ego. She's overwhelmed with the conviction that she's superior to everyone. She possesses a subtle poison, and that poison is pathological self-absorption. This type of mother lacks empathy and isn't self-reflective in any way.

These are mothers who crave the spotlight, even at the expense of their own children. Her own life is more important than her child's. An NM is a mother whose drive for a dramatic starring role in life is greater than the love she has for her child.

These mothers will always make you feel bad, guilty, and ashamed. They'll use their anger and manipulate your weaknesses to get the job done. An NM can make you feel like you're a terrible person, that you're the one at fault for all the bad things that she does.

She'll stop at nothing to make sure someone else is to blame for her actions.

An NM behaves this way because she has an overwhelming drive to feel superior to everyone else. A narcissist believes that they're elevated above everyone else and better than the average person. They have a god complex, a strange delusion of themselves, and believe that they deserve better in life. These beliefs and their subsequent actions can hurt an NM's child, and they may try to cope by retreating into themselves. They can become mentally, emotionally, and physically exhausted.

But narcissists can also display more favorable behavior at times. NMs, for example, can be fun and spontaneous when they want to be. This can be disorientating for people around her. However, despite this, it's important to recognize abuse when it's there. Someone who doesn't show you unconditional love or support is likely to be manipulating you—even if at times they appear to be a good wife or mother.

To overcome and recover from a relationship with an NM requires learning about the narcissistic disorder. Educating themselves will allow the adult child to live without the toxic influences of that parent. It'll teach them that they're an independent adult and not a child. These lessons will put them on the road to recovery and healing.

CHAPTER 3

DETAILED CHARACTERISTICS OF A NARCISSIST

WE'VE ALL HEARD of the word "narcissist." Some of us may know one in our personal or professional lives. Narcissists display particular traits, actions, and behaviors that indicate narcissistic personality disorder (NPD). These traits are commonly described as:

- A grandiose sense of self-importance
- Living in a fantasy world to support their delusional sense of self
- The constant demand for praise and attention
- A sense of entitlement
- Exploiting others without feeling any remorse
- Bullying, threatening, belittling, and demeaning others

Despite outward appearances, narcissists have an incredibly fragile sense of self and deep-seated insecurities. Their disorder acts to overcompensate for this. It becomes problematic, as their need to prop up their idealized, grandiose self-image creates dysfunctional actions and behaviors which are damaging to those around them.

Noting people's everyday behavior and how they relate to and interact with family and friends is essential in determining whether they have narcissistic tendencies. You need to beware of narcissists as they will use and abuse those around them to make themselves feel powerful and validated. A narcissist is extremely resistant to changing their behavior, often blaming other people and denying that they are the one with a problem.

Narcissists are vulnerable to experiencing problematic relationships. People with NPD can't build and maintain normal intimate, work-related, or familial relationships or good friendships. They've too high a view of themselves to allow for reciprocal, unconditional relations built on trust and openness. There are only two types of interactions that the narcissist is capable of: giving orders and receiving them. They had this relationship with their parents, and it's a similar relationship they have with their children.

The narcissist is continually evaluating those around them, viewing others as potential threats or as potential victims. They won't give any personal, meaningful time to anyone. They'll tell other people what to do and expect them to obey. Obedience is the only way someone can maintain some semblance of a relationship with them and ensure that they can continue receiving the narcissist's attention. This pattern of order-and-obey is a regular part of the narcissist's life; it's what they've learned and continue to do. This behavior is how they've survived. If someone has a different opinion or view from them, they immediately become suspicious and hostile.

A narcissist simply can't comprehend that someone may have a different point of view to them. That's why, according to them, they're always "right" in an argument and become so defensive when challenged. The more they're questioned, the more they'll lie to win the fight. A narcissist is incapable of having a meaningful, two-way conversation and is highly sensitive to what they may consider criticism.

Narcissists possess specific characteristics that are difficult for most people to understand. For instance, a narcissist can be intolerant of people's emotions while being very emotional themselves. They lack empathy and compassion and will be cold and distant even with their own children. They also are typically very critical of others. They believe that they deserve to get whatever they want no matter the cost.

An NM will often treat her child the same way that she treats other people; she'll attempt to control and manipulate them from day one. The mother will try to influence the child's mind, body, energy, and soul by any means possible. This will make the child grow up believing that they're not an independent being with their own thoughts.

The pattern will continue as the child gets older, although they'll often become more aware of their mother's behavior. The child will realize that their mother continually tells them what to do. They'll begin to see that they can't do anything on their own, including making their own decisions. The child will believe that they can't be trusted to make appropriate decisions because they've been formed, shaped, molded, conditioned, and influenced by their mother since birth. They haven't been allowed to think or act for themselves. Of course, it's unrealistic to expect everything you do to be perfect, but the child will think otherwise. To them, their mother is perfect, and they'll never be able to live up to those standards. They'll never be good enough.

And it's true to a certain extent—no matter what her child does, it's not good enough for the NM. That's why she should never have been a mother. She's not capable of being a loving parent who lets her child learn and grow from their own mistakes.

An NM can't have a meaningful conversation with anybody, least of all her child. She'll act immaturely, speaking only about herself with no interest in what others have to say. She's the center of her world, and this is reflected in how she converses with others.

This type of mother will try to make other people's lives meaningless in some way or another, especially her child's, to bring value to her own. She'll try to use her child to validate her own life in some way. It involves insidious and constant mind games. For example, an NM has bought her teenage daughter a cheap, second-hand car to replace her old one. She might say, "Do you like this new car I've bought you? It's $200 cheaper than the car you had before. You're going to love it. You're going to love it because *I* love it. You'll love this car that your mom has bought you. Don't you like it? Well, it *is* old. Oh, it's *old*! You know, you can't believe how old this car is. I mean, it's a miracle you can still drive it. But it was cheap, so, you know…"

The mother will subtly use misinformation to make the child believe that they don't deserve, or will never afford to, buy nice things. She'll hammer the point home, ensuring that the child feels that they'll get nothing but garbage in life.

The child will grow up feeling as though they're inadequate. Because the mother is always pointing out how other children get better stuff than them, they'll feel like they're not good enough. This feeling will invariably become part of the child's personality as they get older. The NM will try to make the child believe that there's something wrong with them just to make her feel better about herself.

The NM won't have good things to say about her child, who'll try to understand why and how their mother can be so cold and unaffectionate. They may grow up resentful, albeit successful at being kind and understanding to other people. But they'll always carry the burden of feeling inferior, inadequate, and insecure. They'll never feel good enough for the mother because of her constant spoken and implied assertions about their worth.

The NM doesn't tend to have many (if any) friends, but she doesn't care as it's been that way her whole life. She's self-absorbed, self-centered, and selfish and will tell her child that these are good traits to have. This is another characteristic of an NM—she lives in a world of illusion. She feels that she's more fantastic than she actually is.

CHAPTER 4

TYPES OF NARCISSISM

NARCISSISM IS OFTEN ASSOCIATED with the following personality traits: self-centeredness, extreme self-preoccupation, vanity, selfishness, and egocentricity. These characteristics aren't indicative of extreme self-love; they're manifestations of deep-seated insecurity and the delusions of grandeur they've developed to counter this.

People who've grown up with narcissistic parents have histories of emotional and even physical abuse. It's not hard to see how their parents' behavior can significantly impact their mental health—a reality that they have to deal with every day.

Adult children of narcissistic parents have a hard time coping. They're often filled with toxic emotions that have built up over time. How do these individuals heal their emotional pain and move forward? They need to take the necessary precautions to stop the narcissistic abuse from continuing.

We all know that adults often suffer from guilt, anger, depression, and anxiety. They're all mental states that a child can experience also, and particularly children of narcissistic parents. Narcissistic parents attack the child's emotions and play on their feelings of guilt and worthlessness. They deny them any recognition of their emotional pain. The child learns that their feelings don't matter, and only those of their narcissistic parents do.

If emotional abuse continues, there's only one way out: the child must find the inner strength to move forward and heal their past pain. They're faced with a choice of either numbing their emotions, suppressing their feelings and intellectual growth, or fighting back and taking control.

Narcissistic parents that abuse children often radiate a significant amount of negative energy. These parents have often been abused themselves and don't know how to let go of the pain. They want to leave the abuse behind but take their past and turn it into their negative belief system. The pattern of abuse continues.

The child of a narcissistic parent can't escape the continuous negative energy. This atmosphere can cause severe psychological damage, including depression, anxiety, and fear. The child will feel unsafe, hopeless, and helpless.

If they want to live a happy life or maintain a healthy sense of self, it's impossible to carry on like this. It's time for the adult child of a narcissistic parent to begin the healing process. But this won't be easy. The narcissist doesn't just disappear or change their attitude overnight. And the emotional scars left from their abuse run deep.

Narcissists come in many guises, and by identifying these various types, you'll be able to start to recover from your association with them. You need to understand how the narcissist works and how to deal with relationships involving one. It's also important to realize that the narcissist will weave an intricate web to hook you, luring you into a false sense of security.

There are many kinds of narcissists, but we'll be looking at these three types: grandiose, vulnerable, and compensatory.

Grandiose Narcissism

Grandiose narcissists believe that they're superior beings and are therefore entitled to special treatment. This unrealistic belief system leads them to demand that others idealize them and indulge all their wishes and desires.

Vulnerable Narcissism

Those who have a vulnerable narcissist personality disorder believe that people of the opposite sex are inadequate and beneath them. They think they should put themselves at the top of the hierarchy and have absolute power and control. These narcissists may believe they're superior and choose to treat others as inferiors, wanting them to act subservient to them.

They have a sense of entitlement and expect others to indulge their wishes. They behave self-righteously, with a sense of self-sufficiency and freedom from others.

This sense of entitlement and superiority leads them to violate others' rights as they try to exercise power and control over others. They lack empathy and are indifferent to others' needs and suffering, as long as they can fulfill their own needs and desires. Therefore, the actions of vulnerable narcissists can be deemed antisocial.

Compensatory Narcissism

Compensatory narcissists may take on responsibilities beyond their capabilities as they have an exaggerated sense of their abilities, talents, or skills.

They engage in overachievement to feel better about themselves. These individuals can be domineering in situations where they sense deficiencies in their abilities or talents and may develop grandiose ambitions. They may be overly sensitive to criticism.

These narcissists have a sense of entitlement and superiority and may be preoccupied with fantasies of success. They may believe that they deserve special treatment.

They're vain and are prone to show off their bodies, often making a great effort to elicit admiration from others. They may buy all sorts of useless, unnecessary, or expensive things to feel better about themselves. These narcissists may start sexual activity very early in life and engage in risky sexual intercourse and affairs.

People displaying these narcissistic traits could have a narcissistic personality disorder (NPD). There are several types of NPDs that we'll now briefly look at.

1. Typical Form NPD

This type of NPD involves a relatively healthy mind that's subject to delusions and confabulations. This type of NPD is found mostly among doctors, lawyers, clergy, and academics. More than 85% of people with NPD are women.

2. Long-Term Personality-Changing NPD

This type of NPD has long-lasting symptoms, but the person doesn't receive treatment.

3. Manageable Form NPD

This type of NPD is only visible among socially inept individuals who have deep-seated feelings of inferiority and are willing to acknowledge their condition and consent to some form of treatment.

4. Situational NPD

This form of NPD is present in people who've been subjected to emotional or physical attacks.

5. Labile

This type of NPD is characterized by mood swings in individuals who commonly exhibit erratic behavior.

A More In-Depth Look at Types of Narcissists

Super narcissist

This type of narcissism is a common form of NPD. This narcissistic personality displays a great deal of vanity, both in the clothes they wear and their choice of activities they undertake to show off to the world. Essentially, they're trying to prove that they're the most attractive, clever, and talented person in the room.

The main problem with these narcissists is that they're only interested in the superficial things in life and in keeping up appearances. They'll fill their world with activities and people that are merely accessories to their end goal: looking the best. This narcissism is all about outward appearances and reputation.

The super narcissist continually moves from one activity or friend to the next. They may appear to be extremely busy and have many friends. Still, there's a sense of emptiness or boredom beneath the veneer. They may be very successful and display many desirable traits, but sometimes this belies a lack of personal talent. Their success can often be attributed to other people who work for them or from family connections.

This type of narcissist is usually very charming and will ooze a façade of success. They may be very cunning, allowing them to fool their detractors. The super narcissist also manages to make people feel important while using them for their personal gains. When they're done with them, they'll toss them aside. This narcissist tends only to keep a small core of people around them.

Magnetic narcissist

This type of narcissist can be tricky to spot. They tend to be good-looking and charming and easily draw people towards them. They'll also tend to pit people against one another, paving the way for their own success. This narcissist will make every effort to look attractive to the opposite sex. Once they've won your interest and trust, they'll use you to make themselves feel more confident and vital. Deep down, they've no genuine interest in the relationships they create and will often fake emotion to end them.

The magnetic narcissist maintains their independence and doesn't need people once they're done with them, satisfying their own needs. They're adept at knowing what other people need or want and manipulate this for their benefit. Their success comes from their chameleon-like abilities; they make others think they've found a genuine, unique, and trustworthy friend or lover. The truth is, the magnetic narcissist is incapable of loving or caring for anyone. Another danger is that they can turn angry and aggressive when they feel that they've been betrayed.

Masked narcissist

This type of narcissist will make themselves seem humble and unassuming. They will surround themselves with charming and attractive people. Masked narcissists will make it seem as though they're more interested in their friends than themselves. They use this as a ploy to get others to talk about their problems and then won't give any useful advice in return. If anything, they'll dwell on others' issues, stirring the pot until the other person is left feeling inadequate.

The masked narcissist uses similar covert tactics in their sexual relationships. They'll not use direct or aggressive sexual advances but passive or veiled methods. Often, they'll make others feel guilty for the unwanted attention they've given them and act as though they're the innocent party. They're also adept at using charming behavior to avoid addressing any problems within their relationships and will exploit others for their own pleasure.

This is one of the most challenging forms of narcissism to defend yourself against, as the narcissist is excellent at disguising their manipulative behavior. Even when confronted, the masked narcissist will aggressively deny everything. They may make you feel threatened and put you down, leaving you too scared to face them, or will make you feel guilty for accusing them of inappropriate behavior. The masked narcissist never admits to any wrongdoing and will ferociously proclaim their innocence.

Entitlement narcissist

This narcissist will make everyone think that they're the most important person in the room. They want everyone to believe that they're someone who can do no wrong. This person makes sure that they get their way every time and will look for people whom they can use like servants to achieve their goals. These are narcissistic individuals who use their power to make others feel inferior. Because they make threats if others don't comply, they end up getting away with it.

The entitlement narcissist will take advantage of their superior position to abuse their victims, making others feel like they have no choice or will in the matter. They convince their victims that everything will be fine as long as they do what they're told. The entitlement narcissist succeeds in making others feel guilty and that they owe them something. Others will go out of their way to help this narcissist, often with nothing given in return.

The entitlement narcissist won't take any responsibility for their actions and will always assert that they're right in an argument. They'll empower themselves by any means, whether their measures are appropriate or not. This narcissist type will make you feel like a child and won't be compassionate towards your feelings. They want you to feel how *they* want you to feel. And if you don't, then they'll convince you that you're the problem.

***

All of these three types of narcissists have abusive tendencies. Even the most charming of narcissists will take advantage of people, even when they pretend to care or say they want to help. The narcissist's inherent lack of sympathy and compassion, their false sense of self and reality, their often cruel and manipulative actions, and their inability to recognize their harmful behavior makes it incredibly difficult to live or cope with them.

Regardless of the type of narcissist you're dealing with, you must be brave and stop any further abuse. It's vital that you save yourself from their power plays and set boundaries to prevent yourself from becoming drained mentally, spiritually, and physically. Sometimes the narcissist doesn't even have to be physically present to be manipulating you. The key is to extract yourself from them and start living your own life on your own terms.

CHAPTER 5

DIAGNOSING NARCISSISM

A PERIODIC PSYCHOMETRIC population survey measures personality characteristics' stability over time. Personality tests, including personality inventories, are computer applications that assess personality and personality disorders' main dimensions. To identify narcissistic personality disorder (NPD), psychiatrists conduct physical and psychiatric examinations using these methods to rule out other conditions and determine the most likely causes of symptoms.

If a psychiatrist identifies NPD, they'll also try to determine what environmental factors caused the condition. A therapist will conduct several diagnostic interviews with the person who suffers from the disease.

The patient will be subjected to both objective and projective tests. Once these have been conducted, the therapist will make their final diagnosis. The diagnosis will be used to prepare a treatment plan which will then be put into place. If someone suffers from

NPD, they'll receive a course of treatment designed to help them become better adjusted to their condition.

Unfortunately, it's often difficult to diagnose NPD, as those who suffer from it typically refuse to acknowledge their symptoms and get help for the condition. A narcissist will characteristically believe that it's other people who have a problem and not them. Even with a diagnosis, they may be extremely reluctant to change the behavioral patterns that have more than likely been with them since late childhood.

Narcissism is a mental disorder specific to the abuser and their victim. When you've suffered from narcissistic abuse, it manifests as a hidden mental condition. Narcissistic parents don't let you see how they're hurting you. They treat you like an object, making you feel worthless, as though you're at fault, and that you're a terrible person. You come to feel ashamed of your past and sometimes may believe that there's nothing left to live for.

A victim of narcissistic abuse is shown the dark side of humanity — a dangerous world of damaging emotional chaos. The victim will often try to escape this abuse by not paying attention to it, by blocking it out. They build up mental defenses as a way of dealing with the attacks of a narcissistic parent. But this isn't healthy. If their trauma goes unaddressed, they may risk repeating the harmful patterns of their parent.

CHAPTER 6

THE NARCISSISTIC MOTHER-DAUGHTER RELATIONSHIP

THE DEVELOPMENT OF a mother-daughter relationship in which the mother displays narcissistic tendencies won't follow the same patterns as a so-called "normal" or healthy mother-daughter relationship. A mother typically provides nurturing, unconditional love and allows her child's emotional and intellectual development to flourish. There's no room for this in an NM-daughter relationship where the NM seeks to control and manipulate her child to fit in with her idealized view of herself.

A girl's relationship with her mother starts in the womb. Even the birthing process and the precious hours following it are important moments when the mother and daughter can begin to bond. In the earliest months of her life, a daughter has a special relationship with her mother, whom she sees as a nourishment source. If the mother refuses to bond with her daughter at this stage, it'll sow the seeds for problems later on.

As her daughter develops, the mother becomes the person of most importance in her life. She's the girl's main confidante and adviser. She starts to instill a "gloomy" view of the world into her daughter based on her overreaction to negative events. The NM may begin to manipulate and put down her daughter to boost her own fragile self-esteem. The relationship will be based on many conditions, and the daughter will start to feel smothered and controlled.

The NM will continue to reject any attempts by her daughter to develop a nurturing and stable relationship. She will use her daughter to get back at those who've upset her. She aims to hurt her emotionally and doesn't want her daughter to develop her own personality, thoughts, or beliefs. The NM may see her daughter as a threat and use every means possible to put her down.

There will be little hope of this relationship improving. The NM's daughter will grow up to, at best, feel estranged from her mother and, at worst, resent her. Hopefully, the damage caused by her mother's coldness and emotional manipulation won't have long-lasting effects. However, the aftermath of a dysfunctional relationship such as this *is* likely to result in certain adverse consequences.

Mother-daughter relationships can be a force to be reckoned with, especially when the mother is mentally and emotionally unstable. Daughters of NMs become oppressed by their "loving" mothers and grow up to become women who endure incredible traumas. They may develop negative personality traits, including:

- shame

- anger
- depression
- hesitancy and confusion
- over-sensitivity
- submissiveness

A mother can also instill behavior in her daughter that she learned as coping mechanisms during her childhood. These traits will only serve to harm her daughter in her personal and professional future. The daughter, a repressed version of her mother, may have difficulty holding down a career due to intense anxiety over rejection. Her first relationship might be with an abusive man as she struggles to feel worthy of true love and affection. The daughter, raised by her narcissistic parent, will develop a repressed personality riddled with shame and anxiety. The cycle will go on and on.

Often, the mother, unable to tolerate the idea of her daughter's potential growth, will try to stop her from breaking away. Her inability to let her daughter progress could force her daughter to try and rebel against her. The daughter will know that she's now a woman in her own right and will try to challenge her mothers' authority and perception of reality. If this is thwarted, the daughter may become angry and resentful.

An NM engages in controlling behavior, telling her children what to do, and won't hide her anger or displeasure if she's disobeyed. She's selfish, materialistic, and manipulative. Her own needs are what matters. The NM is incapable of seeing her child as anything other than an object to fulfill her fantasy about herself. She treats her child like a puppet that she can control. Ultimately, she fails in her role as a parent.

An NM will withhold approval or praise and control a child to make sure she gets what she wants. This narcissist will ignore the child and use this lack of attention as a punishment. NMs believe that there's no point discussing things with children because of their inability to understand or reason.

The NM will lie to her children and blame them for any negative occurrence. This behavior can throw even young children into depressive states. Even more damaging is how it'll destroy their sense of self-worth.

If you're the child of an NM, you'll experience a sense of deep sadness. To heal, you need to learn to love yourself because your mother failed to give you positive reinforcement. You need to learn how to forgive yourself for the failings of your mother. You need to move on and let go of the emotional pain.

In adulthood, children of narcissistic parents have difficulty with relationships, mainly because they were made to feel worthless throughout their childhood. This sense of worthlessness makes you believe that there's no point to anything and that you don't deserve healthy, fulfilling relationships based on love and respect.

The narcissist parent expects their child to act in a certain way— to be perfect. They don't see their child as a person in their own right. Their child is an object or a tool for their selfish needs. The parent will be controlling and often display their anger when they don't behave just as they want them to.

The child of a narcissistic parent has a hard time connecting with other people, finding it hard to trust. They'll feel devastated because they want to have a normal life and forge genuine connections with other people. However, they've been made to feel inhuman and may not be able to experience, show, or control human emotion appropriately.

The child of an NM will seldom commit to long-term relationships and carries a burden of emotional pain inside them. They don't want to risk feeling unloved and rejected and may even feel as if they're still being used and abused as they're repeatedly living with their past. The child of a narcissistic parent will always feel ugly and unworthy but can't see how their past abuse has shaped their thoughts and personality. They don't realize how their negative thinking patterns result from their relationship with their NM.

A relationship with a challenging parent has a profound impact on a person. That person will be made to feel unsafe, alone, and empty inside. The child learns to survive by doing what they're told and pray they get it right, although they're often told that they haven't. There's no affection, praise, or encouragement. They find it hard to derive pleasure from the things they do.

The average mother feels like she's doing a good job if she nurtures and looks out for her child mentally, emotionally, and physically. Her child doesn't have to be the "perfect" daughter. She cares about her child and loves them unconditionally. She wants to give her child the tools to live a happy and successful life.

On the other hand, an NM will make her child feel worthless, neglected, unsafe, abandoned, and used. The NM doesn't care about the child's future; she only cares about having the perfect child to show off to the rest of the world. The child lives in fear because they feel like they must always please their mother.

A sad fact is that the child learns to accept their mother's behavior. They feel they have no control over the situation and may even blame themselves for not being the ideal daughter.

However, suppose you recognize some of these behaviors in yourself as a mother or in your partner. In that case, it's essential to know that unhealthy narcissistic patterns can be broken. It'll be possible to have a healthy relationship with your child based on boundaries, respect, affection, and consistency.

It's vital to set up boundaries with your child and respect each other's roles in the relationship. Your child feels safe and secure when they appreciate you and understand your nurturing role as a parent. You need to give your child affection, to show that you care, and for them to know that you love them unconditionally. You must allow your child to express their love for you and not deny them their emotions or feelings.

You must show your child that you're okay with them doing their own thing. They're not there to please the mother. Be approachable and let your child know that they can come to you if they've any problems. Don't make them feel like they're being scrutinized or criticized all the time.

It's essential that narcissistic parenting is recognized and stopped before it's too late. Otherwise, the damage caused will have a lasting effect. The victim will end up feeling unsafe, alone, and misunderstood. They'll carry with them a sense of being emotionally abandoned. Their personality becomes molded into something that isn't them because they've been controlled in an abusive and manipulative manner. The child of an NM will feel confused and afraid of everything. They'll blame themselves for their past abuse and for all the problems they now face.

The biological connection between a mother and a daughter is hard to break. Whether healthy or harmful, that bond will have a lasting impact on the daughter as she navigates through life in her personality, relationships, and decisions. Without the comfort, love, affection, or guidance of a good mother, the child of an NM will find life hard and empty.

CHILDHOOD EMOTIONAL NARCISSISTIC ABUSE

A narcissistic parent uses their power and advantage to emotionally beat down their child and take away all their rights. The child will become confused, hurt, scared, and even depressed. They'll feel alone, trapped, and with no one to turn to.

The only things keeping these children from hurting themselves are the coping mechanisms they develop to distance themselves from the abuse. They've no hope that the abuse will stop, so they mentally and emotionally "guard" themselves. Each day they're threatened with being expelled from the home, having their life destroyed, or even being killed. This feeling of unsafety in their environment is too much for a child to have to deal with.

When someone tells you that they'll hurt you, you believe them, giving them the upper-hand. The narcissist wants complete control, so they'll use threats and say whatever it takes to get their way. NMs use guilt and fear tactics in this way to control their children. They make the child believe that it's best to endure the emotional abuse as the alternative is likely to be worse.

The narcissistic parent will never show compassion and say they're sorry for the pain they've created in the past or the pain that they'll inflict in the future. They can hurt the child at any time and not take responsibility for doing so. An NM doesn't care about their child's emotional well-being and can't show sympathy or offer their child stability. They're only concerned with power and don't care if the child suffers. Their child's emotional pain is considered to be a necessary casualty.

The narcissist parent doesn't care about their children's rights, identity, or independence and will try their best to take these away from them. The child becomes dependent on their narcissistic parent and devoid of their own personality and opinions.

It isn't easy to escape the abuse of an NM. As a child, the torment is often a daily occurrence. Even when the child eventually leaves home, they'll carry the pain with them. The narcissistic parent doesn't show concern for the person they're abusing or have abused and will even punish their child for trying to talk about it. The narcissist is a sick, twisted person who needs professional help, and their child feels like a prisoner in their own home.

The abused child is trying to hold onto their life in a toxic environment. Often, they'll feel completely alone and unable to confide in someone about what they're going through. NMs can come across as charming, and this may lead others to disbelieve what the child is telling them is happening behind closed doors. Sometimes other family members will be complicit in the abuse or too scared of the NM themselves to confront her.

The child has to discover how to clarify what's real and what isn't, and this is something they'll have to do on their own. Their NM is living in a fantasy world and hasn't provided them with a true sense of reality. The child must understand that their parent will never change. In the meantime, to fit in, the child will often take on some alter-personality to appease their abusive parent. The child must go through tremendous anguish to fully heal from the mental and emotional mistreatment.

The child needs to understand the abusive parent's dual-personality. Their NM doesn't have the capacity for real love (even though she may have pretended to show it). The child needs to understand this horrible truth and try to forgive themselves, to realize that it wasn't their fault they were treated that way. They need to comprehend that this was abusive behavior and that it wasn't warranted.

Children of NMs can suffer lifelong effects from the abuse, and it'll take hard work and determination to heal. They'll need to experience and work through all the emotions brought about by coming to terms with what's happened to them. It's difficult for many people to understand the pain inside an abused child's head. They suffered daily and for many years. If this pain isn't addressed, it may lead to mental or personality disorders, which will worsen with age if left undiagnosed and treated.

Being in a constant state of emotional pain is a powerful feeling. Sometimes, this can lead to suicidal thoughts or tendencies. Other times, the child may try to turn the pain into anger, leading them to feel even more out of control and helpless. A child may end up mimicking the behaviors and disease of their abusive parent.

Sometimes a child develops a split personality to cope with childhood abuse—a toxic mix of their abusive parent and healthy self. It's an entirely separate person from their true self, and you'll never know where you stand with them.

The abused child learns how to protect their real self, often isolating themselves and avoiding friendships or relationships. They feel as though they have to watch what they say and not reveal their true thoughts or feelings. They're hard on themselves. In some cases, they'll fake their emotions if they think that's what others want them to do. A child with an abusive parent is living a lie at all times.

It's a real-life nightmare that they feel they'll never escape. The abused child's mistreatment has been so severe that they derive little pleasure or joy from life. They're fragile and have learned to mistrust people for fear of getting hurt further.

However, outwardly, the abused child can seem happy even when they're feeling depressed. They've learned to stay quiet, to disguise their pain, and to deal with their problems alone. The child may be afraid to confide in others as they feel defective, that they've caused their abuse somehow. But they're vulnerable and filled with pain, and without help, they may find it impossible to heal.

The child has to learn to be selfish at times, to take care of themselves, and forget about upsetting their parents or others. They need to become self-reliant and push their way into the world as an independent, free-thinking individual. In doing so, they'll forge a new life for themselves and may be able to help others in the same situation.

Taking a stand for what is right will save the abused child. As they start to heal, they may have difficulty trusting anybody and will need to get better at letting people in. They'll have a hard time feeling safe and secure as they're still fragile and damaged from the horrific abuse that's been forced on them. But they need to realize that their voice needs to be heard, that they *will* be understood. They're unique and strong individuals who can rise above the destruction of their past.

* * *

And what about the abusers? What are some common characteristics that narcissistic parents share? These abusive parents tend to be overly-critical, over-controlling, inconsiderate, lacking in compassion, empathy, and the ability to display love and affection. They don't care about others, only themselves. They're incredibly self-centered and egotistical and will stop at nothing to get their way. When they feel they've been let down or betrayed, they'll react in anger or try to shame their child.

Narcissists are a danger to their families as their actions and behavior will have long-lasting, harmful effects on their children. On top of their narcissistic traits, NMs may have substance abuse problems or other addictions, leading to violence towards their children. It's improbable that an NM will seek professional help as narcissists live in a fantasy world where they can do no wrong, and everybody else is the problem.

It's a sad fact that those who've been abused may turn into an abuser. That's why those who identify as having lived with toxic parents must seek help to stop the cycle of abuse from further damaging their lives and those of others.

It's challenging living with an NM. You'll lose your identity in her shadow. Envy, jealousy, and rage are common symptoms of NMs when their daughters refuse to accept them as the head of household. The NM will force the child to become a reflection of her inflated self-perception. If the child fails to live up to the narcissist's standard, then they'll be treated in a cold, uncaring way. They'll be made to feel shame and embarrassment. The NM will victimize the child for not paying enough attention to their well-being. The NM's controlling nature and her unrealistic demands will create guilt and shame.

The NM will give her child "gifts" (what others would call childhood necessities) as compensation and to prove that she is, in fact, a caring mother. The child will feel guilt for thinking badly about their mother in the first place. This type of emotional abuse is incredibly destructive and will have far-reaching consequences.

The Damage Caused by Narcissistic Mothers

Many daughters have relationship problems with their mothers from time to time. However, with NMs, there's no room for discussion, compromise, or resolution to these problems. An NM will say that their daughter is being difficult and will manipulate her into thinking that any issues are the daughter's fault. The daughter will doubt herself, and the cycle of destructive, abusive behavior will continue.

Many adult daughters of NMs will feel inferior to others as their mother always chose themselves and their immediate family before the daughter. The daughter was manipulated into thinking that her mother was better than her, that she'd never reach her standards. The daughter becomes hypersensitive, feeling that she's not good enough, useless, and undeserving of love or praise.

Many daughters of NMs perceive their mothers as unloving and cold. They believe their mothers pay them attention simply because she wants to be in control of them. To make her children feel guilty for thinking this, the NM will show "love" by doling out gifts as compensation. These so-called gifts are often no more than essential items, but the NM will make a great fuss about her generosity.

Daughters of NMs will feel unloved—not just by their mother, but by everyone. This lack of affection may cause them to act in a more sexually aggressive or seductive manner for attention. NMs manipulate others to get what they want. Their daughters may find themselves doing the same without knowing why they're acting that way.

The daughters of NMs will always compete with each other. NMs will gossip about their daughters, and this affects their daughters' lives. Some daughters react by being rebellious, while some will be clingy and over-dependent. These daughters need to learn to overcome their addiction to their mothers.

How to Cope With Your Narcissistic Mother

A daughter of an NM will need to learn how to stop the emotional abuse caused by her mother and the feelings of victimization she now inflicts on herself.

NMs will make you feel bad about your flaws. You need to learn to stand up for yourself, to be assertive, and to express yourself. You also need to realize that your feelings, needs, thoughts, and accomplishments are valid.

The daughter needs to understand how her NM has made her feel. She'll need to recognize and be aware of her feelings to discover how her mother impacted her mental and emotional landscape.

The daughter needs to search deep within herself to overcome this abuse and learn it's okay to speak her mind. By asking herself the right questions and by seeking help from professionals and other survivors of narcissistic parenting, she'll be able to see how her NM abused her. In turn, the daughter will gain strength in her convictions, and she'll be able to start making healthy choices.

The daughter will need to stop believing what their NM told them about themselves and life. She'll need to start labeling her mother as an "abuser" and as someone who didn't have her best interests at heart. The daughter will need to examine how her mother's words and actions have affected her. She'll need to discard everything her mother taught her to believe about herself and discover how to restore her self-esteem and self-worth.

Now the daughter will embark on a voyage of self-discovery. This path to healing will require empathy, not just for herself but for her NM also. She'll need to realize that her NM isn't capable of compassion and will have to understand how this impacts her and how to let it go.

The daughter will need to stop allowing others to control her, including her NM. She'll need to learn to be assertive and communicate effectively, including how to express her thoughts and feelings appropriately. She'll need to know when to speak and when to listen.

Once the NM's daughter learns that narcissists are incapable of unconditional love, she'll realize that she was never truly loved by her mother. This revelation will be tough, but the daughter will come to terms with the fact that her mother suffers from an illness and that she wasn't to blame for her coldness and distance. When she's at peace with this, the daughter will be able to move on with her life.

Over time, the daughter will learn that she doesn't have to stay a victim and can enjoy healthy relationships without manipulation, pain, or fear. She'll realize that she needs to love herself first and be happy to be alone until she meets someone who accepts her unconditionally. The daughter will come to believe that she's no less a person because her mother was narcissistic. She'll be able to leave the prison created by her NM and live life on her terms. She'll no longer need to have her NM in her world.

How the Narcissistic Mother Punishes Her Child

The ultimate goal of the NM's punishment is to make her daughter feel bad about herself and make herself feel good. Daily, she'll give her daughter the message that she's worthless. The NM will make a great effort to make sure that her daughter is subservient to her wants and needs.

An NM also punishes her daughter by giving her negative attention. For instance, she may react melodramatically to any criticism her daughter gives her. Or she may give her daughter the silent treatment if she's been disobeyed. The daughter will believe that their mother will only love them if they're the perfect child.

An NM will continue to emotionally abuse her daughter while giving a false impression of caring about her. She'll present herself as the perfect mother but will only show kindness when beneficial to her.

As she's incapable of genuine empathy, the NM will only act sympathetic when she wants to "reward" good behavior. The rest of the time, the NM will be cold and unfeeling or quick to anger when her daughter has displeased her. The daughter will resent her mother for her lack of empathy but won't be able to express this.

Not every NM is the same, but what they all have in common is their inability to love their daughters or show them empathy or compassion. As they try to mold their daughter into a self-reflection of their grandiose self-image, an NM will neglect the fundamental norms and principles of motherhood.

Having a Narcissistic Mother: The Emotional Impact

When they leave their NM, the daughter will feel that she's finally free from the emotional tyranny forever. This is a wonderful development, and we can only be overjoyed for people who leave an abusive or toxic environment.

BUT! The hardest part is yet to come. What lies ahead is a grueling emotional marathon and possibly the most significant challenge the daughter has ever had to face.

The daughter must face an overwhelming, intense emotional struggle to overcome the emotional and mental enslavement that attaches her to her narcissistic parent. If she doesn't confront it, she'll experience excruciating emotional pain for the rest of her life and run the risk of taking on some of her NM's narcissistic traits.

She has a strong emotional reliance on her mother and often her father as well. She sees them as two super-powerful emperors in her life. She idolizes them for their intelligence, devotion to family, and integrity.

It may take her years to realize that her mother isn't who she thought she was. Through a process of self-discovery, she'll determine that she had been tricked and deceived. She'll find that the notion of her mother as a superior, perfect, loving being was just a myth.

The realization will hit her like a potent drug, shocking and paralyzing her body and mind. It'll feel like being kicked in the gut and falling straight to the ground. The emotional pain that's unleashed can seem catastrophic, like an immense earthquake breaking the ground underneath her feet. The emotional response is real and terrifying. The daughter realizes that her life has been based on lies, deceit, and manipulation.

The important thing here is for the daughter to take care of herself. She needs to seek professional help and talk to people who can minimize the damage caused by her past. She needs to try her best to be positive and remember that she deserves to make a life for herself. Most of all, she needs to distance herself from her mother while she heals and not let her know that she feels broken, lost, or unstable.

CHAPTER 7

ADULT DAUGHTERS OF NARCISSISTIC MOTHERS: AN OVERVIEW

THE ADULT DAUGHTERS of NMs have to deal with the trauma of being brought up in a narcissistic, toxic environment since birth. Even when they've finally left home, the fallout from their upbringing will have a long-term impact on their personality and relationships. These daughters will need to embark on a voyage of self-discovery and re-birth, possibly with the help of therapy, to stop their past from impacting their present and future. Here are some of the issues which may afflict the daughters of NMs once they've left their family home.

Withdrawing From Relationships

Daughters of NMs will often find it hard to stay in relationships. Growing up with a narcissistic parent has made them fearful and insecure. On the one hand, they're afraid of being alone as they haven't learned how to be independent or trust their instincts. On the other hand, they're scared of having no safety net if they fall or something to cling to if they're pushed away. In this sense, the daughters have a hard time getting close to other people.

These daughters have a hard time falling in love as they feel like they have to be on guard all the time. This feeling isn't just because of the pain and trauma they've experienced in their childhood; they also feel they have to hide the truth about their NM. The daughters feel unworthy of love and affection, tainted or damaged goods from being brought up in a toxic household. They won't have the capacity to trust or become attached to anyone. They'll feel conflicted, as they *want* to have a normal relationship, but it may seem impossible to them. As a result, they'll end up feeling even more insecure.

Anger and Rage

The daughters of NMs will experience anger and rage, often from an early age and throughout their lives if their past isn't addressed. As a child, she possesses feelings of helplessness and anger at the oppression and manipulation she experiences. She feels that her family doesn't love her. As the daughter gets older, she may threaten to leave every time there's a dispute. She'll start to question every aspect of her relationship with her NM and look for ways to escape her. The daughter will be critical of every action of her mother and find it difficult to forgive her.

This anger or rage will continue for the daughter even when she leaves home. A daughter of an NM will harbor resentment at how she was treated and won't want her mother anywhere near her. If the daughter has children of her own, she'll make every effort to keep her mother away.

It's easy to see how the daughter's anger is justified as she was (or still is) living in one of the most emotionally manipulative and controlling relationships possible. The mother would continually tell her negative things to damage her self-esteem and self-worth. The daughter was lied to about everything. She had no choice but to go along with the lies and manipulation. It's no wonder that she's left with the desire to lash out and blame her mother for a life that was unfair and unjustified.

If the daughter of an NM doesn't address these feelings of hurt, anger, and resentment, she may become bitter and mean-spirited, impacting her future relationships and interactions. In this way, even after she leaves her mother, she'll still be under her influence.

Daughters of NMs can take this anger and use it as a positive force to get healthy. By recognizing their feelings, they'll be able to get help for the abuse they've experienced. With therapeutic input, the daughters will realize that anger and resentment are a trap. They'll learn to stop blaming their mother and move on.

Anxiety and Depression

Emotionally abusive relationships can cause the victims to suffer from anxiety, depression, and low self-esteem. Living in a constant cycle of abuse, manipulation, fear, insecurity, and lovelessness damages your mental and emotional health. The abused will end up feeling helpless, hopeless, unworthy, and with the sense that they're trapped in a world that they can't get out of.

CHAPTER 8

THE EFFECTS OF NARCISSISTIC PARENTING

THE DAMAGE DONE BY a narcissistic parent on her child will depend on the level of narcissism going on at the time. Still, generally, all children of NMs will feel controlled and manipulated to a certain extent. The children will feel as though they have no independent choice or thought, which may affect their ability to find healthy relationships later on in life. It's understandable how someone raised by an NM may become bitter. But children brought up in a narcissistic environment are survivors and *can* take back control to experience joyful and fulfilling lives.

Narcissistic parents can be devastating. They're masters of manipulation and gaslighting, and it can be impossible to see the abuse for what it is while you're growing up. However, as an adult, it's possible to recognize the narcissistic abuse inflicted on you, even if they're good at covering their tracks. Each person's experience of having a narcissistic parent is unique. You may have experienced some or all of the following issues having been raised by one.

Low Self-Esteem

Narcissistic parents tend to pick on the things they dislike about you, what they perceive to be your flaws, and amplify them. As a result, you may develop low self-esteem, be self-effacing, or even feel useless and unworthy.

Trust Issues

It's normal to have trust issues after being raised by a narcissistic parent. You may feel that you're never good enough and that nobody could love you for being you. Your parent's erratic behavior and cold manner will be a blueprint for how you see others. It's difficult, but it *is* possible to overcome these issues and rebuild trust with others.

Lack of Empathy

Because of their issues with emotions, narcissists often don't experience empathy. They also tend to lack feelings of remorse and guilt. Since you were raised by a person who doesn't feel or recognize emotion the way an average parent does, it can be challenging to understand your feelings. However, you're not at fault for your parent's lack of compassion and shouldn't blame yourself for their inability to care about you.

Codependence

Because a narcissist uses their children as a source of narcissistic supply, this can end in codependence. Narcissists use their children in ways that will reflect well on them (like encouraging them to play certain sports) or push them into activities to show them off. Simultaneously, a parent with narcissistic personality disorder (NPD) will use their child as an emotional punching bag. You may have been trained to take care of the parent first and foremost, without any regard for its impact on you.

Shame

Many people who grow up with NPD parents experience shame in one form or another. Your parent may have criticized you for everything from your appearance to your school performance and social life. You may have a strong sense that you're never good enough for anyone.

Low Self-Worth

Suppose you want to thrive after growing up with a narcissist. In that case, it's essential to recognize that you're not worthless simply because your parent couldn't healthily love you. You're valuable and worthwhile as an individual. You deserve to be happy, and there are things you can do to make that happen.

Always look for the good in yourself. It can be hard to see your worth, especially when your parent consistently expressed doubts or openly criticized you. It's important not to lose sight of your good qualities. Remember that the way your parent treated you was their issue and not yours.

Emotional Flashbacks

People raised by narcissists may experience emotional flashbacks triggered by a word or a situation that reminds them of the bullying inflicted by their parents. These sensations are a normal part of healing from emotional abuse. You may experience these flashbacks and have no idea why, or you may be able to recognize that it's coming from a place of pain caused by your past.

Poor Self-Image

It's typical for the child of an NPD parent to have a poor self-image and see themselves as "less than" other people. However, it's possible to rebuild a healthy sense of self and move past the low self-worth by coming to terms with the abuse they suffered.

Isolation

Narcissistic parents often isolate their children from other people. The parent may see other people as competition for resources and attention or be jealous of their child's time spent with others. You may have been forced to socialize with other adult relatives who had the same issues, and your parent might have made out that something was wrong with them. You may have grown up with the sense that people are "bad," as your primary role model would have been your toxic parent.

Social Withdrawal

A narcissist's child will learn that other people hurt you, so it's safer to avoid them altogether. They might be afraid of being rejected or humiliated by others. It's important to overcome this fear, especially if you want to build future healthy relationships.

Fear of Abandonment

Narcissistic parents have a way of making their children feel afraid that getting close to other people will leave them alone and abandoned. The narcissist will make sure that they're always present when other family members or friends are with the child. They may even make the child feel like they're the reason people are nice and friendly to them.

It's essential to realize that you've done nothing wrong and aren't to blame for the abuse you suffered. Remember that you're not alone—others have gone through similar experiences, and many of them have been able to heal and move forward with their lives. If you're ready to move on and leave behind the pain of the past, consider getting help from a therapist. You might also find it helpful to talk about your experience with a friend. If you're ready to work on healing from narcissistic abuse, you deserve support and compassion. Talking and listening to people you trust will help you step into a healthier future.

A helpful way to start recovering from toxic parents is to learn to love yourself. It's vital to find someone you can talk to and who'll listen to you and give you good advice. This person needs to understand how you feel and make you feel like you're not alone. Find someone you feel safe with (a friend, therapist, family member), and don't hold back. You deserve to be heard.

EFFECTS OF NARCISSISTIC ABUSE: BEYOND CHILDHOOD

Emotional abuse can affect adult children long after childhood, and these effects can be devastating. Many adult children have learned to detach from their emotions and trauma bond with their parents. Adult children of narcissists need to discover how to take control, set healthy boundaries, and appropriately process their feelings.

Forced Emotional Detachment

Adult children of narcissistic parents can exhibit symptoms of forced emotional detachment. These feelings can be very confusing for them. These children run the risk of developing a borderline personality disorder, a complicated condition with various symptoms. These symptoms include a pattern of unstable relationships, identity problems, unstable self-image, impulsive behavior, fear of abandonment, self-harming behavior, suicidal behavior, lack of empathy, and a distorted self-image.

Learned Helplessness

Learned helplessness is another disorder that goes hand-in-hand with narcissism. The children of narcissists are put in an environment where things are frequently changing and over which they've no control. This upheaval means that the child is left feeling helpless. The child isn't heard or listened to and feels unconnected to the parent. This experience can be very confusing, and the child will feel stuck in a "one-way relationship." They won't know how to give love and how to connect with others.

Becoming a Narcissist

In clinical psychologist Albert Bernstein's book, *Emotional Vampires*, he explains how narcissists' children can become narcissists themselves. He says that these children "can feel superior and special when they put others in pain. They have been through so much pain themselves that hurting others may feel right." These children are confused about how to deal with the relationships in their life. Narcissistic parents often destroy childhood innocence. When these narcissistic children grow up, they try to look perfect, but they have a fragile self-image.

Learning to Cope

Adult children of narcissists can leave the relationship and not have any contact with their parents. Or, they can remain in the relationship and attempt to form a more egalitarian, less dependent relationship with their parents. They can create a co-dependent relationship whereby they give to get. Giving to get is known as a quid pro quo relationship. The adult child gives themselves to one parent so that the parent gives them simple things like love, approval, and nurturance. They can do self-destructive things for the sake of keeping the peace. Or they could simply try and pretend that nothing is wrong.

They can remain in the relationship and take care of one parent while allowing the other parent to stay out of sight/out of mind as much as possible or at least out of any real contact. They can engage in therapy, learn about narcissistic personality disorder and develop appropriate boundaries.

Adult children of narcissistic parents are often left with having a hard time trusting. They usually don't know how to love or trust themselves or others or even believe that they're worthy of being loved. But these children can find ways to cope with their symptoms.

Getting engaged in self-care is vital to start the healing process. Getting connected to support groups and self-help workshops where they can share their experiences and feelings will help on the journey to self-discovery. Learning about narcissism and how to protect themselves from the red-flag behaviors of narcissists is also important. They need to take care of themselves, detach themselves from their narcissistic parent, and be firm. They need to be grateful for who they are and to take the time to learn about themselves and to forgive.

Learning About Narcissism

Learning about narcissism can be very helpful to adult children of narcissistic parents. A massive sense of relief can be gained from finally understanding what makes narcissists the way they are. They can learn about second-hand feelings and how to get these feelings under control. They can discover how to restart their self-esteem and have healthy boundaries with others. Most significantly, they can understand that they weren't to blame for their parent's behavior and learn not to repeat the same narcissistic patterns.

Communicating

Communicating with a narcissist can be dangerous. In many cases, adult children of narcissists have learned to read between the lines to make sure there's no risk of them displeasing the other person. They know to do this to survive, but this can be harmful to them in the long run.

Many adult children of narcissists have learned to "detach" to cope. Detaching from people by not caring enough to listen or engage with them will lead to a lonely life. This detachment is often seen in adults who've been through immense trauma in their childhood.

Children have to say "no" to have healthy relationships. Saying "yes" by accommodating the narcissist's every need and anything the narcissist wants can interfere with healthy relationships in adulthood.

Managing Feelings of Emptiness

Managing feelings of emptiness is an issue for many adult children of narcissists. This feeling often stems from the lack of security provided in childhood. These children can feel very unsure of the world and often have trust issues. They often can't grasp why the narcissist doesn't love them or like them. As the narcissist feels empty inside, this generates a profound effect of second-hand emptiness in the child.

***

A Short Message From Happiness Factory

Hey, are you enjoying the book? We'd love to hear your thoughts!

Many readers don't know how hard it is to find genuine reviews and how much they help an author.

We'd be incredibly grateful if you could take just 60 seconds to write a brief review on Amazon, even if it's just a few sentences!

Thank you for taking the time to share your thoughts!

Your review will genuinely make a difference for the author and help gain exposure to our work.

CHAPTER 9

THE ABUSIVE NARCISSISTIC MOTHER: SYMPTOMS, CAUSES, AND HOW TO RECOVER

IF AN NM RAISED YOU, you probably lived through immense emotional suffering as a child. It's important to realize that you weren't at fault—your mother was the problem—and now that you're an adult, it's time to heal. Identifying the damage your mother caused and making sure it never happens again is an integral part of that process.

SYMPTOMS OF NARCISSISTIC MOTHER SYNDROME

First, we have to understand why a person would be emotionally or physically abusive towards their child. NMs are narcissists, and this means they must have complete control over all things. This control is achieved through abuse of one kind or another. NMs will use their children to get what they want, including financial gain, to feel good about themselves.

The narcissist is continuously looking for "supply" to fill their inner void caused by low self-esteem. This constant demand for "supply" (validation and gratification) means that they must control every situation to benefit from it. These benefits include adulation, praise, admiration, or anything else that a person desires from someone else to make themselves feel good.

When a child is born to an NM, they automatically become a "supply" source. As the child grows older, they'll be manipulated into carrying out their mother's every whim. This manipulation is usually done in some covert way to avoid detection. An NM will be sure not to hurt the child in any way that would draw unwanted negative attention.

The NM will keep their child under control by using covert and overt methods of abuse. Covert methods include brainwashing, gaslighting, and other subtle emotional manipulations. Overt forms include verbal abuse.

Perhaps you're reading this because you've suffered from precisely these forms of ill-treatment yourself. A narcissistic parent will often be dismissive, critical, or even verbally abusive towards their children. They'll put their needs before the requirements of their child. You may have been afraid to get close to your mother because you feared her turning her back on you at any moment. If you look back, you may be able to identify the times this happened in your childhood.

Many children raised by NMs struggle with their self-esteem because of the constant criticism they endured growing up. Often, this criticism was designed to make the NM feel better about herself. NMs may also compare their child to others, especially other family members, whom they consider to be more successful in some way or another.

If you grew up in a household controlled by an NM, chances are you were emotionally abused. She probably used emotional tactics like guilt or belittling you so that she could feel better about herself. You might have had to put her needs before your own for her to love and accept you. Your mother might have made you feel like you were never good enough, and this may have made it hard for you to develop healthy self-worth.

It's common for people who grew up with an NM to suffer from codependency issues as adults. They might find themselves in relationships with other abusers because they don't know any other way or how to leave the relationship or set healthy boundaries. A child who grew up with an NM might think they're responsible for others' feelings and actions. They might not recognize that the other person's behavior is out of their control and something they can't change.

If your mother was a narcissist, you probably felt like she didn't love you. If you look back, you may be able to spot the moments when she used "love" as a punishment or reward.

The symptoms of narcissism often take a while to surface because a narcissistic parent can hide behind their "nice" mask for some time. They may also be able to put on a show of love for the sake of appearances. As children get older, they begin to notice that something isn't right. They may start to sense that their feelings don't matter or that their needs aren't significant.

CAUSES OF NARCISSISTIC MOTHER SYNDROME

An NM will usually be emotionally distant from her children. She may seem more interested in her own needs and wants than the needs of her children. This kind of mother may also be emotionally manipulative and will often use guilt to control her children.

Narcissistic mother syndrome is a serious psychological and personality disorder. It's a complex issue and can be strongly influenced by a wide number of factors. The exact causes aren't entirely known, but some factors include:

- attachment issues in childhood
- family dysfunction
- exposure to drug or alcohol use in childhood

Other research shows that narcissism may be caused by genetic factors predetermined before a child is born. It's also likely that the child of an NM will display narcissistic traits in later life.

Diagnosis of NPD is difficult without medical intervention. A doctor will need to carry out physical and psychological tests. Often, narcissists are the last people to admit they have a problem and need professional help.

The main characteristic of an NM is their apparent high self-esteem. However, this isn't an accurate depiction of their mental state. The mother's self-esteem is, in fact, very fragile and highly dependent on external validation and self-deception. This is why she'll use her child as a way to gain self-worth, just like a vampire sucks blood from his victims.

When you're in a relationship with a narcissist, it's common to feel confused. You'll feel as if you're on an emotional roller coaster. They'll tell you that they "can't live without you" while simultaneously making you feel worthless. Your instincts may tell you that they're lying and manipulating you to make themselves feel better. Still, they'll make you feel guilty for thinking this.

If you've lived with an NM, you probably feel your past has negatively impacted your present in some way. You may feel the shame and guilt from your childhood holds you back and that you can't move forward. You must remember that you *can* move on from your childhood, but it will take courage, strength, and persistence.

RECOVERING FROM NARCISSISTIC ABUSE

The effects of these abusive behaviors can be massive. Someone who's been abused by their NM will feel like something is missing inside of them. This emptiness might compel them to search for help to understand who they are away from their narcissistic parent.

The child of an NM has been made to feel that they can never measure up to their mother's expectations. This results in low self-esteem, potentially leading them down a path of self-destruction. They'll have little sense of identity, have no idea who they are as a person, and feel lost and alone.

Narcissistic abuse tends to cause hypersensitivity; the victim will always be alert for criticism. They were often told by their NM that they weren't good enough. Because of this hypersensitivity, they'll have difficulty relating to other people or feeling secure around others.

Survivors of narcissistic abuse may develop trust issues and experience PTSD symptoms, making it hard for them to find and maintain relationships. Even in a loving relationship, they might still be plagued by their NM's voice inside their head, telling them that they're not good enough for that person.

The children of NMs have difficulty trusting others because they were abused by someone who was supposed to love them unconditionally. They'll often wonder why anyone would love them and think they're different from everyone else. Their experience was indeed different to many, but they're not abnormal.

If you've suffered from an upbringing with an NM, you need to understand that you're okay just the way you are. You don't have to be a slave to your NM's voice that's stuck in your head. You can learn how to silence this part of you and live the life that you always wanted.

You can heal from the abuse and move forward with your life. But the only way to do this is to understand fully what your NM did to you.

Recovering from narcissistic abuse isn't easy, but that doesn't mean it can't be done. We'll give you all the information you need to get started on this path. We'll explore how to begin recovering. We'll also talk about the steps that need to be taken to accomplish this.

If you want to recover from your NM, you'll need to begin by facing the reality of what your childhood actually was. This can sometimes be a complicated process. You may feel guilty about the way you were treated growing up, especially if it happened frequently.

It's important to realize that you're not at fault for how your mother treated you. It can be hard to accept that you were hurt by her, especially if she seemed so wonderful on the outside. If your NM could keep up a good appearance for other people, it might be difficult for others to believe the things you tell them about her.

An NM can be very damaging to a child, especially if she was emotionally abusive. It's important to realize that you weren't the problem. You can begin the healing process by looking back and learning that your feelings were valid and that what she did had nothing to do with you or your worth as a person. There's no reason to feel guilty about the way she treated you. She wasn't a good enough mother, and you don't need to be a good enough child.

If you're close to your mother, and she's worked on herself as a person, you're in a great place to move forward from. It's essential to understand that the type of woman she is now has nothing to do with the kind of woman she was when you were a child. You need to separate the two to heal.

You might find it helpful to look for support from others who have gone through similar experiences in narcissistic households. Talking to other people can be valuable in your healing process. Your friends and family members may even be shocked to hear the things you have to say, but all of it's valid, and they'll probably be supportive.

You should know that recovery isn't going to happen overnight. It takes time and effort on your part, but you're worth it. You can find ways to move forward from the person you were into the strong person you want to be. It all starts with acceptance of the past and being willing to take the steps needed to heal.

Facing Your Narcissistic Mother

If you're looking to face your NM, you need to be prepared for the emotional roller coaster that awaits you. Even if you have a good relationship with her now, the abuse you suffered may come back to haunt you as soon as she opens her mouth.

Saying No to Her

When facing your NM, it's important to remember that she'll probably want something from you in exchange for her love and acceptance. Your mother's need for control may also re-emerge.

Your mother might be upset when you tell her that you don't want her in your life anymore. She may be surprised and think that your relationship was fine. You need to be ready for the emotional consequences of making this decision. Your mother might get angry or overly-emotional. She may try to make you feel guilty, or she might try to manipulate your relationships with other family members to get you to back down.

You can distance yourself from her without completely severing the relationship. You may not want her in your life today, but that doesn't mean you won't want her in your life tomorrow. Nothing is fixed; you're in control of your choices and decisions according to your needs and feelings. Don't let her get to you—you've made your decision, and it's time for her to deal with the consequences.

If your mother is a narcissist, she probably has a whole list of people she blames for her pain. You're likely to be somewhere on that list. She might blame you for some event that happened when you were very young, or she may tell you that you were the source of all her problems and misery growing up.

If you decide to cut contact with her, she undoubtedly has a list of reasons why you're a terrible person. She'll say that it's all your fault for distancing yourself from her. The truth is your mother might be living in denial if she can't admit that she's the source of her pain and yours.

There's no reasoning with a narcissist. If she tells you that it's your fault she has problems, just remember that you're not responsible. She can't even take responsibility for her own life, so why should you be accountable for it?

Your mother might try to control your life to get what she wants. It's important to understand that this is her problem, not yours. She has to take responsibility for her own life choices, no matter how much she tries to blame you for the things that she can't control. You need to stay focused on your feelings and goals, even if your mother does everything in her power to get you off-track.

Reclaiming Your Life

It's time for you to stand up and say no to your NM. You're responsible for living your life, not her.

If you were emotionally abused as a child, you need to understand that the past is in the past, and there's nothing you can do about it. You can't change your mother or the things she said to you. All you can do is take responsibility for yourself and the things that are happening to you in your life today.

You can begin to heal by separating yourself from your NM and her negative influence. Don't let her guilt you into thinking it's all your fault. It's time for you to take control of your own life.

You need to realize that she probably suffered from narcissistic abuse growing up. NMs often come from narcissist abusive households, so you need to remember that it's not your fault. You didn't cause her issues—she brought them with her into this world, and it's up to her to do something about them.

It's time for you to start standing up for yourself. Your NM can't hurt you if you don't let her. She doesn't deserve to get the things she wants from life by harming others, and you no longer need to sacrifice your feelings for her to feel better about herself.

It's easy to blame someone else for your problems, but the truth is you're responsible for your own life. Your mother can't control you, no matter how much she might try. It's time for you to set boundaries, leave the past behind, and focus on living a happy, healthy, and fulfilling life. You deserve it.

CHAPTER 10

MENTAL MANIPULATION AND CONTROL BY NARCISSISTIC MOTHERS

HERE WE DISCUSS SOME behaviors, words, and actions that an NM will use to manipulate and control her child. If you recognize any of these, you could have been brought up in a narcissistic household. You may need help to recover your mental health and prevent the cycle of abuse from continuing.

Belittling

This is a simple yet effective trick an NM uses to manipulate her child. The aim is to make their child feel like they are a failure in life. The shame and sense of unworthiness this tactic produces enables the NM to control her child's actions and thoughts.

Attacks

Just like an animal, the NM will attack, not so much physically, but with words. Her verbal attacks are meant to hurt and belittle her victim, making them feel powerless.

Avoidance

This is a passive-aggressive way of punishing her children for some perceived transgression or simply because she's had a bad day. She'll ignore her children and pretend they don't exist.

Bait and Switch

The NM will promise her children something positive (a vacation, a privilege, etc.), and then when the time comes, she'll decide she doesn't want to go through with it. Or if her child does something for her, she'll promise a reward but then decide that it isn't worth it.

Condescension

The NM will look down on her children and tell them that they're too young to understand what she's talking about. She'll also put down other people who are successful or happy to make herself feel better. She tends to be jealous of others.

Drama Queen

Everything with an NM is a drama. Every situation is exaggerated, and every action taken to fix it escalates it instead of resolving it. Things are always made out to be worse than they really are.

Exaggeration

The NM will tell her child about someone or something and make it out to be far worse than it actually is. It's a way of using fear to manipulate.

False Accusations

These are meant to isolate the child from other people and make them feel as though they can't trust anyone else but her. The child will begin to think that everyone else is talking about them and that they're unliked or unloved. The NM may even accuse others of doing the things that she does.

Lying

Lying is common among NMs, from small, white lies to perjury. They tend to be very good at telling lies that paint an untrue picture to gain sympathy or admiration. However, they can easily get caught in their lies because they'll accidentally tell the truth or contradict themselves within the same story.

Narcissistic Rage

When an NM is called out, called to account, or even just asked a direct question, she'll often become enraged. She may go on the attack verbally, or if cornered, rage and scream and throw things. This is because, deep down, NMs live with an empty feeling of self-loathing and shame. It's why they try to make everyone else feel as bad about themselves as they do.

Favoritism

An NM will play favorites among her children, giving special treatment to control them or their behavior. That child will be expected to live up to her expectations and do what she wants, or they'll be told, in no uncertain terms, that they have failed. She may also ignore a child completely and pretend that the child doesn't exist.

Emotional Blackmail

An NM will use emotional blackmail to get their child to do what they want. The parent will give a demand disguised as a request. Suppose the child doesn't acquiesce to this. In that case, the NM will punish them through passive-aggression, sulking, shows of anger, guilt-trips, withholding possessions, and even violence. This behavior is dangerous. It teaches the child that they've no control over their situation, that they can never say no, and that their boundaries will never be respected.

The NM may even threaten to kill herself if the child doesn't do what she wants. Or she may threaten to hurt the child or someone else. Sometimes, she'll threaten to reveal something that she has "found out" about the child to get them to comply with her.

Use of Fear, Obligation, and Guilt

The NM will use fear, obligation, and guilt to guilt-trip their child into doing what they want them to. Consequently, the child will feel that their own needs and rights don't count and that they have no free-will. They may feel guilty about making choices later on in life.

Shaming

NMs will continually shame their child, making them feel flawed and worthless. They do this so that the child will be more compliant with their requests and demands. The child will feel powerless and is likely to carry this feeling into adulthood.

Triangulation and Compensation

By constantly comparing their child to other siblings or children, the narcissistic parent aims to belittle them, make scapegoats of them, and make them feel unworthy. By playing children off each other, the parent will instill an unhealthy sense of rivalry and make their child fight for their approval.

Gaslighting

Gaslighting is a classic tactic used by manipulators to make their victims feel disorientated. They'll feel as though *they're* in the wrong and not their abuser. Gaslighting entails the distorting of reality and facts and the denial of any abuse taking place. It's a method which has long-lasting effects as the child can grow up doubting themselves.

You must know that you don't have to deal with narcissistic family members. You can stay away from people who don't treat you how you deserve to be treated. It's important to practice self-care and self-love and undo the damage caused by your NM's behavior, words, and actions.

Everything we've mentioned above can adversely affect the child of a narcissistic parent long after they've left home. They will need to actively seek help to reverse the effects caused by their childhood's toxic environment.

Suppose you don't face up to this toxic past. In that case, your NM's negative behavior and comments will affect your friendships, relationships, and work. With forgiveness, understanding, and self-love, you can break the patterns which left you feeling worthless, helpless, and tied to your NM's every whim and desire.

You need to stop blaming yourself for your parent's disapproval and actions and come to terms with the fact you'll have to re-learn what you know about the world. You'll come to understand that you're allowed to have your own thoughts and feelings, that you have free choice and free will, and that you don't have to pander to other people to feel loved or accepted. You'll be able to live a life filled with self-acceptance and love with no feelings of guilt or shame.

CHAPTER 11

NARCISSISTIC STRATEGIES OF MANIPULATION

IF YOUR MOTHER IS A NARCISSIST, you must remember that you're not alone. NMs come in all shapes and sizes and come from a variety of backgrounds. But they all use particular manipulative strategies to get what they want. Studies show that females tend to fall for these tricks more easily than men. Males find it more difficult to relate to the narcissist's behavior rather than get manipulated by them.

This chapter describes some of the manipulation tactics used by mothers with an NPD. The first five outlined here are the most commonly deployed strategies used on both the NM's child or adult-child.

Mind-Reading and "You Should," "You Ought to," and "You'd Better."

NMs can accurately read their children's psychological vulnerabilities. Their children usually feel pressured to do whatever their mothers tell them to do. Perhaps the most popular narcissist strategy is known as "mind-reading." An NM's child is programmed to believe that whatever their mother is suspicious, upset, or angry about is correct, accurate insight. The mother can create a web of fictitious lies about her child's selfishness, vices, and immoral behaviors and persuade her child of how bad they are. For instance, if she suspects the child of being materialistic, she'll accuse them of this and then repeatedly tell them they shouldn't be that way. She'll frequently tell them they should be more sensible with money or give some of it away.

The mother will demand that the child stop being so controlling, selfish, and domineering. She may even tell them they should stop taking advantage of other people and not be so sensitive. All of this is projection: when people project their bad behaviors onto others in an attempt to convince themselves that these negative traits aren't theirs. When a narcissist suspects her children of immoral and unethical conduct, she persuades them to act in a particular manner. Thus, the narcissist gets her way while her children believe that her suspicions are valid.

"You get what you deserve" is another common phrase used by NMs. The children of NMs start to believe that they can't do anything right because their mother is continually telling them what they should do. Her children have to always be in line with what *she* thinks is right. Otherwise, their NM will make them feel guilty and ashamed. She'll question her adult-child over why they don't give her grandchildren, why they've no ambition in life, or tell them they've no values and never help anyone in need. In her mind, her children are no good, and they shouldn't be that way. She demands that they be "perfect." She may even compare them unfavorably to other siblings or family members, saying, "Why aren't you like them? They never gave me any trouble. Your sister is so much better than you."

"You're Nothing Without Me."

NMs will imply this whenever they feel threatened or are trying to preserve their position of authority or superiority. This strategy can also be a powerful tool for her to suppress her children's development. For example, suppose her daughter was to become successful. In that case, the mother may translate this into a threat to her authority and undermine her daughter's success. So, she may even want to hurt her daughter or make her feel ashamed and inadequate. The NM may demand that her children give her their earnings so she can invest them for them. She may suggest that they live off her income. She may assert that she's entitled to her children's success because she worked so hard when they were little and deprived herself of things for them. Her children may believe her, and they may feel ashamed and guilty because she makes them think they should give her gratitude for their success.

Selective Memory and Abuse Amnesia

Abuse amnesia is a defense mechanism used by narcissists to escape accountability for their actions. NMs will recount past incidents with such conviction that their victims are left questioning whether the abuse ever occurred. Victims of narcissistic abuse often experience bouts of memory loss when trying to recall specific incidents of abuse. Their narcissistic abusers typically employ a "dissociative defense mechanism," which is also commonly referred to as "spacing out" or "zoning out." Narcissists purposefully use this tactic to gain a position of control.

Many narcissists "space out" during conversations with their children who are trying to express their feelings. To make their children feel uncomfortable, vulnerable, unsure of themselves, or to distract them from the true nature of the abuse, the narcissist temporarily withdraws from the conversation and acts confused and perplexed. The NM somehow finds it difficult to recall the events that have caused her children to suffer. Sometimes she may say that she can't remember what she said or what she did.

However, most narcissists typically remember the events they've carried out with great detail and clarity. When she's confronted, the NM has no difficulty rationalizing her abuse. Sometimes she'll admit her guilt and apologize. But this will be given in an ambivalent and insincere way. By saying that she's sorry for her child's treatment or for being a bad mother, she seeks to regain power and control over her child. She may also hint at the fact that her child is the one who's in the wrong.

Victims of narcissistic abuse are trained by their NMs to believe that they don't know what happened. The mother makes her children feel that it all happened by mistake, by accident, or by circumstance. She may be very loving when she's not abusing her children, so they assume that the other times she mistreated them were a mistake. When the children encounter problems in their lives, the mother will deny any part of it. She'll somehow manage to persuade them that they're the root cause of their misfortune. The children start to blame themselves, and they feel ashamed.

The mother may say, "I did that for your own good. You're such an ungrateful child. Look what you've done." Again, this is the mother projecting onto her children. She's trying to turn the blame for her misdeeds onto them. The children start to believe that they're wrong or have done something to cause the abusive act. They won't question her when she says things like, "I neglect my children because they didn't care about me. They do that to me on purpose. They take advantage of me," "They don't appreciate me. They don't know how hard I worked for them," "They don't do anything for me," "They left me alone to go out and party all night," "I spent all my money on them, "I'm never good enough for them."

Victims of abuse spend a great deal of time figuring out whether the abuse was their fault or not, and the mother benefits from this. So, if the children start to believe that they're the ones in the wrong, they'll blame themselves, and they'll feel ashamed of themselves. The mother tries to compensate for her guilt, shame, and remorse by making her children feel as bad as she does. In other words, she gets them to carry out her abuse for her. When younger children ask why she treats them that way, she'll blame them and tell them it's because they're in the wrong. She uses her children to justify her misdeeds because she always has to be right. So, the children become her scapegoats; she can't blame herself, so she blames her children instead.

Denial

NMs are aware of the hurt and damage they're causing, but they can't empathize with the consequences. So, the NM will affirm that she never said what she said or that she never did what she did. An NM will deny the abuse and refute claims that she's a troubled person. The children may try to figure out whether what she's saying is true or false, but they end up confused and with no definite answers.

Projection

NMs project their feelings, emotions, and motives onto their children. They blame their children for their negative behaviors, and they make their children feel guilty, ashamed, fearful, abandoned, and angry. The children are blamed for what the mother does because she reflects her bad behavior onto them. She may say that her children treat her the same way that she treats them. In this way, the mother can write off her children's complaints as if they were ungrateful for all she's done for them.

If the children complain that the mother abuses them, she may say that the children are doing the same to her. She seems to be saying, "My scars mean nothing to me, and so their scars mean nothing to them." She'll deny her abuse and gaslight and manipulate her children into believing that "it never happened."

Love Bombing

NMs can be very creative in getting their offspring to love, admire, and think about them. One tactic is repeatedly claiming how much she loves her children and grandchildren and how much they mean to her. The NM might shower them with gifts and write cards telling them how much she cares. She tells her children how "wonderful" she thinks they are, that they're "amazing," and that she loves them with all her heart. It's all just a form of bribery to get the child to do what she wants. There's no sincerity or genuine feelings involved.

An NM can be a very sweet, charming, funny, and caring person when she wants to be. But she's inconsistent, and any love she shows is calculated and conditional. In return, the love her child shows her will be conditional also. The child's affection will be based on their mother's behavior towards them. When the NM is mean, nasty, and abusive, her child will reject her. She may say, "I can't stand it," "I hate her," "She's evil and vile, and I want nothing to do with her."

When the mother feels rejected by her daughter, she'll throw a fit and a tantrum. She'll threaten her daughter, "I'll disown you…I'll leave you…it's not going to work." But when she calms down and wants to reclaim her harmonious relationship with her child again, she'll send her flowers, write her letters or make phone calls. So, the child is always on tenterhooks, feeling as though they're dealing with a fragile, impulsive, and fickle person whom she can't fully trust.

Baiting the Other Parent

An NM may use her children to hurt and abuse her spouse. She'll try to make them fight with her spouse because she has to be the victim. She may attack her spouse in front of her children, making them fight him on her behalf. She makes her children feel they can't support or sympathize with their father. In other words, she sets up a "pro-mother" campaign.

She'll make them feel that they have to support her instead of him. She'll instill the idea into her children's minds that their father doesn't provide enough for her, doesn't love her enough, or doesn't do enough for her. The children will feel that their father is the bad guy and that she's the victim. The father will be attacked in this way repeatedly.

The mother will usually listen to her children's conversations about their father, sometimes even secretly recording them. The NM may use them as confidants and tell them things that he's done wrong. She may even turn them into "spies" who report back to her about her husband's actions. Her children will always have to speak to her first before their father.

In this way, the NM has the power and control in the family. She makes her children feel that they have to choose between her and their father, therefore harming their relationship with him. As a result, they may not feel close to him and decide that he's a bad father, relying instead on their mother for parental guidance.

Banishing the Other Parent

An NM might also psychologically abuse her husband. She'll accuse him of being a terrible husband and father or claim that he's psychologically sick or an addict. She may even banish him from the family, either kicking him out of the house or getting a divorce. In this case, the NM will tell her children to have nothing to do with him anymore because of his so-called lousy behavior and character flaws.

The children may agree with her because they're inexperienced, not knowing that she's manipulating them. They're unsure whether she's telling the truth or not but trust what she's saying because she's their mother. They don't know that smearing people's reputations is evil. So, they believe that their father is the wrongdoer and have to do something about it. They start to take sides and feel that they have to protect their mother.

Control

The NM is very controlling. She's a controller of the truth through her lies, secrets, omissions, distortions, and false interpretations. She thinks that telling the children what to do is "right." She says that "children should never disobey their parents." The NM will direct her children on what to do and how to think, controlling their thoughts, feelings, and actions. If the children disagree with her, she'll create a scene and threaten them with words like, "I'll cut you off—I'll have nothing to do with you ever again."

An NM will try to control her children by making them dependent upon her. She'll make every decision for them, from telling them whom to marry and when, what job to have, how much they should earn, how much they should save, what they should wear, how many children to have, and when to have them. She'll tell them what their rights are and what they shouldn't do. If her child is dependent on her, the NM can influence them and mold them into exactly how she thinks they should be.

Hurt and Rescue Situations

A hurt and rescue scenario is similar to love bombing. A period of abuse is followed by one of reconciliation. It creates an atmosphere of codependency and uncertainty. Often, an NM will engineer these situations to assert her control over her children and her spouse. If the parents eventually separate, it gives the mother a better opportunity to manipulate her children further.

In many cases, the husband or father feels helpless. He finds he can't protect his children from his wife's psychological abuse. So, he decides to leave the family. The children will then have to treat their mother as their savior despite her destructive and brutal actions. The mother's possessiveness and control will make it very hard for the children to live comfortably, but they won't have any other options.

Invalidation

The NM will invalidate her children's experiences because, otherwise, it would force her to face up to her wrongdoing. Invalidation is one of the cruelest manipulation tactics. She'll say things like, "That never happened," "It didn't happen like that," "I never did/said that," "I was never like that," "You're lying," "You're making it up," "It didn't happen the way you're describing it."

An NM may deny the existence of the abuse that's occurring in the family. She may say that "Relationships don't work like that," "I don't need to talk about it," or "I don't want to talk about it anymore." She'll tell the children, "You don't know what you're talking about," "You're just a child," "You're too young to understand this," "I refuse to believe you," "Everything is always your fault."

The mother will prevent the children from improving their lives. Instead, she'll defend herself against the truth. For example, she may say, "You don't have bad feelings," "You don't have bad days," "You don't have bad experiences." The NM will tell the children that they're not being abused. Instead, she'll blame them for anything that goes wrong in the family to justify her behavior.

Projecting Faults

An NM will project the blame from her behavior onto her children. She'll say things like, "You asked for it," "If you hadn't done that, I wouldn't have done that to you." She'll discuss her behavior by using the word "you:" "That's because *you* made me do that," "*You* made me do it." Deep down, she's ashamed of her behavior (although she never admits it), and she tries to hide it by blaming her children. She'll label them as cruel, mentally disturbed, and even psychotic.

Gaslighting

As mentioned previously, gaslighting is a cunning tactic used by NMs to manipulate their children into doubting their own experience. This manipulation occurs on an ongoing basis to hide the mother's abuse. NMs use gaslighting to destroy their children's self-esteem, as a form of control, as a fear tactic, and make their children dependent on them. The abuse caused by gaslighting can destroy and ruin someone's life and may lead to conditions such as PTSD.

Abuse of Authority

Freedom for a child is the ability to make their own decisions, to be able to say what they want, to be able to speak up. The NM will abuse her authority by taking these rights away from her children. She'll continuously tell them what they can and can't do, won't listen to them, and will refuse to let them express their thoughts and emotions. This abuse of authority is incredibly damaging to a child's sense of identity and self-worth.

Confusing Conversations

Often, the child of an NM will be embroiled in ongoing, confusing conversations with their mother where they don't get a chance to get a word in edge-wise. It often feels like the conversation is going around in circles. The mother will be babbling, and it'll be hard for the child to understand what's being said.

These conversations usually arise when the mother has been confronted with her behavior and has started to panic. She'll deliberately talk quickly and continuously change the subject and skip from topic to topic to confuse the child and distract them from her mistreatment.

CHAPTER 12

NARCISSISTS AND THEIR LIES

NMs ARE PATHOLOGICAL LIARS. They lie to make themselves appear better than they really are, sound intelligent and caring, manipulate, gain attention, and make themselves feel superior. Their lies can be to cover themselves, blame you, and make themselves seem like the victim.

Because the narcissist is pathological and compulsive, they lie even when the truth would sound better. They lie when they want to win an argument, even when it doesn't make sense. They enjoy lying. It makes them feel powerful. They are the ultimate con artists. They have lived their whole lives entangled in a web of lies.

Narcissists lie to induce guilt. They lie as a passive-aggressive ploy to make you feel bad, and it works. They'll even tell a white lie to make you feel bad. They'll say, "I'm fine," when they're not, just to make you feel guilty for not being able to read their mind. You try to make everyone happy, but you're never good enough.

The narcissist's lies are not innocent. They're not small fibs. Most of the lies the narcissist tells are in the service of getting what they want, getting out of the responsibility of consequences, or making themselves seem worthy in some way.

They can tell the most outrageous lies and expect you to believe them and not question them. Narcissists will lie to you about things that happened only they would know; they'll lie about your past; they'll lie about your family's past; they'll lie when there's no reason at all to lie. They seem to do this for the sheer pleasure of lying. Many of the lies they tell you won't be remembered, and when confronted with the lie, they'll say they don't remember saying it. This is especially prevalent with persuasive manipulators who use the "gaslighting effect" on their victims.

The NM will build a tangled web of lies that grows ever more complex and difficult to unravel. Lies are not just told within the immediate family. It's possible that the lies extend over years and somehow incorporate people outside the immediate family. It's not unusual to find out that grandparents, aunts, uncles, cousins, teachers, and others were involved. And if there was money to be had, even the family pet may have been involved somehow.

The web of deceit may seem to have nothing to do with the narcissist, but more can be learned by watching the lies. Hidden secrets can sometimes be uncovered, and family secrets can be unraveled.

Many narcissists tell lies to protect themselves, to gain sympathy, and to gain attention. Liars can be easily manipulated. But if you know the signs, you can avoid their deception.

Disabled children are prime targets for gaslighting, as their inability to defend themselves makes them quite vulnerable. Disabled children's disabilities are frequently "forgotten." When discussing a disabled child, the narcissist may forget the disability or claim it doesn't exist. The NM will frequently blame the child's disability for the child's bad behavior. In this way, the narcissist gains sympathy and empowers themselves.

The narcissist may say that the child's disability is the cause of grief to other family members. By convincing others that the child is "bad" or "good" or assigning traits to the child, the narcissist gains control over others' perceptions of the child. The NM is saying anything about the child to get power and sympathy.

The narcissist may claim the child is "naughty," "nice," "bad," "good," "a discipline problem," "perfect," and so on to manipulate others into seeing the child in the way the narcissist sees the child. Children are more dependent on their parents' view of them than they can ever be on their children's view of them. The narcissist exploits this to their ends.

The narcissist may lie about the child's sexual behavior, background, etc., to gain power and sympathy. Suppose the child is shy, immature, or sensitive. In that case, the narcissist may induce guilt in others by saying that the child is "too sensitive" or saying the child "can't take a joke." The other family members may then feel sorry for the child. Children are very vulnerable in these areas, and feelings of guilt may continue into adulthood. The family may also continue to tease the child this way, as the narcissist sets the example.

The narcissist may lie about the child's school performance. It's not uncommon to find out that the narcissist lied about the children getting excellent grades or receiving academic awards. The reason for this will usually become clear later on. The narcissist may say the child was attending an exclusive school or receiving special tutoring to gain sympathy.

The NM may claim that the child is very artistic, a genius, exceptional looking, or carries the family "gene," making the child superior. As the NM tends to have an inflated sense of superiority, they'll try to display this as much as possible. By attaching these "superior" qualities to their children, they are integrated into the narcissist's standard of superiority.

The narcissist will manipulate others by taking credit for the child's achievements. Narcissists are great "power-trippers." They will take credit for anything they can and exaggerate the truth. This makes it difficult to know what is real and what is not. It becomes confusing to know whom to believe and who to trust.

The NM may also use the child to make herself look good. This can apply to anyone who doesn't want to look bad for themselves or others. The narcissist may say that the child is better than them or better than children his or her age. But an NM won't help their child. Narcissists take better care of themselves than of anyone else.

The narcissist may not love their children—or anyone, for that matter. They may never have known what real love is, yet say they love you and that their children are "their life." Be careful about taking these statements seriously. If your life is the love of the narcissist's life, you're in trouble. The narcissist will spare nothing to protect their reputation, no matter what the cost.

Narcissists will lie to conceal their crimes. Narcissists are "swimming in sins" and will say anything to cover these up. Don't believe what they tell you until you know the truth. Narcissists may lie about any area in which they feel guilty or ashamed, and they'll also lie to conceal their anger.

Narcissistic rage is a giant black hole that they're almost afraid of. It's been built up over years and years. Narcissists are filled with so much rage and anger that they fear someone will find out about it. Their victims are often treated as "predators." The narcissist will obsess over how to deal with you if you find out their truth. It's more beneficial for them to pretend to be nice than show their enraged face.

The narcissist may not have been mentally abused as a child but still suffers from low self-esteem. "Low self-esteem" is a subjective term that can mean different things to different people. In this context, we're referring to low self-esteem as a symptom of narcissism. NMs with low self-esteem are very tenacious. They're hard to shake loose once they have a grip on something. They're much like a python that can "hug" things to death.

These people make sure they have the best of everything and are not easily let go. They are always looking for an "edge" or something to give them a competitive advantage over others. They get angry if someone else gets something they see as valuable.

NMs envy others. They have a sense of entitlement. They see their needs and wants as more important than others. Narcissists with low self-esteem are highly manipulative. They want to be seen as "good" people whenever they get the chance. This is a massive problem as they'll employ the "white-lie" manipulation method to present themselves in the best possible light. They'll take advantage of any situation they can to make this happen.

CHAPTER 13

THE THREE STAGES OF HEALING FROM NARCISSISTIC ABUSE

THE HEALING JOURNEY FROM narcissistic abuse is a long one, but each stage will help bring you closer to healing. The road may be rough, but the destination is a life of contentment and pleasure.

Stage 1: Shock, Denial, and Isolation

After suffering narcissistic abuse, you may try to deny what happened or blame yourself. You may feel shocked that someone could treat you like a doormat or like a piece of garbage. You might feel isolated and have a sense of loneliness. You might be in extreme emotional pain or confusion. The good news is that these feelings are normal, and they'll pass with time.

Stage 2: Anger, Fear, and Pain

At this stage, you may experience intense emotions and even feel like you're going crazy. You might feel alone and afraid the pain will never end. You may be angry at the narcissist and be consumed by revenge fantasies. You might be afraid to trust again. This is natural! Allow yourself to feel your emotions, experience them, and move through them. The second stage of healing is trying to regain your sense of sanity. Soon you'll become stronger and more resilient.

Stage 3: Empowerment, Adjustment, and Closure

When you progress to this stage, you gain the ability to manage your emotions healthily. You recognize that you're loveable and worthy. You can make peace with the past by forgiving yourself and move forward to build a brighter future. The past abuse won't define who you are anymore. You'll learn from your mistakes and move on without losing yourself. You'll achieve a higher level of self-esteem and self-confidence. The third stage of healing can last a lifetime!

Key Points for Healing

Here are the best ways to get started and speed up the healing process:

1. It's essential to do something about your situation as quickly as possible. Take any action you can to make your life better.

2. Remember your self-worth. Don't let the narcissist's abuse control you and define you. You're so much more than a victim.

3. The more you practice self-care, the better you'll feel.

4. If you do anything painful or difficult, don't compare yourself to others, beat yourself up, or punish yourself.

5. It's important to understand that you have a difficult task ahead of you. It'll be worth it in the end.

6. Remember that you should be kind to yourself and say something positive to yourself every day. It'll help you know that you can be worth the time of loving people around you.

7. If you feel helpless, seeking professional help and talking to other people is okay.

8. You may find it helpful to connect with other survivors on social media and read their inspiring stories.

9. Don't expect yourself to be "normal" or act your old self again. Give yourself time to heal.

10. Take steps in the right direction, and never give up hope that you'll overcome your past trauma and abuse.

CHAPTER 14

A NARCISSISTIC MOTHER: FALSE SELF AND ENMESHMENT

CERTAIN SITUATIONS CAN BECOME so painful and overwhelming that we unknowingly become entrapped or enmeshed by them. This feeling of entrapment happens when you've lived with an NM who's taught you to see yourself as less-than, inferior, undeserving, and flawed. She made you feel this way to bolster her own grandiose, false sense of self.

NMs' abuse is often inflicted covertly through intimidation, manipulation, and emotional invalidation. As an adult child of an NM, your sense of self was shattered by someone who was supposed to nurture your growth and protect you from harm. You've become enmeshed in a false self-image of yourself and feel as though you can't escape.

To overcome enmeshment with an NM, it's essential to:

1. Know the difference between healthy and unhealthy relationships.

Healthy relationships are reciprocal. They're based on mutual respect and not doing things for each other just for personal gain. A relationship with an NM is rarely reciprocal in this way.

An NM is likely to keep her adult child enmeshed because the more she can control her child, the stronger her sense of false self. She needs to be depended on to maintain a sense of self-importance. To overcome their enmeshment, the child will need to detach themselves from her. She won't easily let this happen as she needs her child for self-validation.

2. Take a more in-depth look at yourself and your NM.

An adult child of an NM might recognize they share certain common traits with her. These may include a sense of entitlement and exaggerated feelings of self-importance which belie a fragile ego. You'll need to dig deep into the darkest corners of your mind and see if you, too, hold these personality traits.

It may be painful, but you'll need to confront your past enmeshed with an NM. What were her typical behaviors and actions? What did she say that was harmful or unhealthy? How did it make you feel?

3. Talk with people who understand what you're going through.

Connect with others who've been there, people who've experienced toxic parenting. Talking and writing about your childhood can help you piece together the information into a coherent whole. Engage with others who are willing to hold you in their hearts without judging you so that you can learn how to validate and love yourself.

You'll begin to understand why you felt so much pain while enmeshed with your NM. When you realize that your memories aren't distorted, and you're not defective for having these feelings, you'll feel less alone and isolated.

4. Talk with a qualified therapist.

An excellent way to get support during this process is to start psychotherapy with a therapist familiar with the complicated dynamics of children of narcissistic parents. They'll help you to recognize that the abuse you experienced at your mother's hands was not your fault. If you're still entangled in a relationship with your NM, you'll not be able to make a clean break on your own. Therapy with a compassionate and understanding therapist can help you let go of your pain and embrace the fullness of your being.

5. Allow yourself to feel pain and emotion.

You'll find yourself on a path of grief and mourning for the loss of what could have been. Allow yourself to be angry, grieve, and channel your pain into positive action.

6. Forgive yourself.

The child of an NM will often feel guilt, shame, and responsibility for the abuse they suffered. You must learn to forgive yourself and to know that the abuse was not your fault. Your NM is a flawed individual who thrives on control and manipulation to feel better about herself. What happened to you could have happened to anyone—you're not at fault.

Remember that you can overcome enmeshment with an NM and create the life you were meant to live, free from her and the effects of her abuse.

CHAPTER 15

SEPARATION FROM A NARCISSISTIC MOTHER: THE PATH TO HEALING AND RECOVERY

ONE OF THE MOST CHALLENGING obstacles any child has to face is separating themselves from their mother. Throughout the nine months in utero, the souls of a mother and child are intermingled.

The Baby-Mother Bond: The Dysfunctional Narcissistic Mother

A chemical bond forms between the two that's unbroken until the birth process. This bond creates a sense of security for both mother and child. It also promotes empathy between the two and creates a strong foundation for the child's ability to form intimate adult relationships later in life.

When a child is separated from the mother at birth, bonding must begin again. For most people, this process starts within the first few hours or days after delivery. For others, it takes several months to form. The old saying goes that it's just because some children take longer to bond than others. But in reality, this isn't true at all. Some bonding may seem to take longer because of an unhealthy environment. The child will receive less sensory information and, as a result, won't experience the bonding process as quickly as others.

Most newborn babies spend their first few hours with just their mother. This special time together helps to facilitate the bond between them. It also ensures that the child will receive all of the nurturing, love, and support they need to develop healthy ways. But this isn't always the case. There are many instances in which mothers aren't emotionally available during this bonding period. An NM may be so consumed with losing her own identity that she rejects her child and refuses to bond with them.

There are also instances where mothers bond with their children in negative ways. Because NMs lack empathy and connection to their infants, they may feel inadequate or threatened by the experience while bonding with a child. They may try to deter the child from attempting to connect to protect themselves.

An NM might avoid bonding with her newborn because other family members' presence is too much for her to handle. Some NMs don't believe in bonding with a child right after birth, thinking that the bond will be formed in due time. They may even decide that the family should leave the hospital without seeing or touching their newborn.

Some NMs may feel inadequate or incompetent once they've given birth to their child. They may even want the child to bond with someone else, believing that they're not good enough for their child.

They may even feel jealous because of the amount of attention the new baby is receiving from medical professionals. This jealousy then seeps into their interactions with others in the family and with her baby. Some NMs will leave the hospital prematurely as their feelings of envy and bitterness overcome them.

Another reason for delayed or absent bonding is if the mother has had a traumatic birth experience. Previous miscarriage or stillbirth, or even a difficult delivery, could contribute to this and can create fear, rage, and helplessness in an NM.

Negative emotions arise when the mother isn't supported during labor. The NM may have had complications during pregnancy and the baby's birth, which weren't satisfactorily resolved. She may also have had a lack of support from her partner or her family during this time.

Therefore, there are many reasons why NMs may neglect to bond with their newborn children right after birth. A variety of negative experiences can cause an NM to feel this way. They may be unable to trust their ability to bond with a child and feel fear and uncertainty.

They may be worried that they'll be unable to take care of a newborn child properly. These NMs may be so consumed with the idea that motherhood is an impossible task that they shut out their emotions entirely. They can't bond with the child because they're scared of the experience itself.

Some NMs are so consumed with the idea that motherhood is nothing but work and drudgery that they can't bond with their child. They look at the experience as one step up from slavery.

As many NMs may have low self-esteem, they fear that the child won't love them or that they won't measure up to motherly expectations. The NM may also not bond with a child because of how she was treated as a child.

Many NMs didn't receive what they needed and deserved from their mothers. They may have been neglected as infants or children and didn't experience proper nurturing, love, and affection. This deficit has left them feeling empty and worthless.

Perhaps the NM doesn't feel worthy of experiencing motherhood, which causes them to reject their child. They may think that their past experiences are so painful that motherhood will bring up negative emotions from the past.

Some NMs can't bond with their children right after birth because of the extreme trauma they experienced as a child. They may have been neglected or physically, emotionally, and verbally abused by their mothers. This experience has left them feeling like they never had a chance at the motherly experience.

They may be afraid that going through the bonding process will only open up old wounds that are still healing. They don't want to re-live the pain that they felt as a child. Some of these NMs may have felt like they were born into a kind of hell, impacting their current-day motives and thinking.

***

Being separated from their NM after birth will result in various effects on the child's psyche. Some of these are only temporary and disappear after a short period. Others are more long-lasting and can endure for a lifetime.

It's important for those separated from their NMs after birth to process this experience for themselves. While difficult, it will ultimately be therapeutic. The first step is to acknowledge that there was a separation, a fact that they may have been in denial of or had little knowledge of.

There are a variety of reasons why people may deny something like this. They may feel that acknowledging the separation makes it more real. But it's vital to recognize the truth about any problematic situation to process it and move on.

People who experienced this separation may feel like they didn't have a fair chance at the motherly experience. They must come to understand how processing their feelings can help them. Processing feelings is healthy and safe if they're discussed in a structured environment. People who've not processed their feelings may have difficulty talking about the experience and will carry feelings of injustice and unfairness.

Processing your feelings is also an excellent way to deal with anger and hurt. No one deserves to be neglected or treated with cruelty or abuse, especially after birth. People who've not processed their feelings about the separation may be at risk of self-destructive behaviors.

Some people may cope with their pain by harming themselves or others. They might act out by using drugs or alcohol to numb the pain. They may also become addicted to activities like gambling or pornography as a distraction from their emotions. It's best for those who were separated from their NMs after birth to try to process their feelings so they can begin to move on.

People separated from their NMs after birth need to understand that there was a reason for this separation. It may or may not have been unavoidable at the time. Finding the cause is a significant step in processing their emotions.

An NM's child may feel sadness, anger, fear, grief, or a sense of abandonment when they try to work through this issue. They may feel as though they weren't good enough for their mother, and that's why their NM left them. They may feel hatred toward their mother for abandoning or neglecting them as a child.

People who were separated may also feel guilty about things that aren't their fault. They may feel guilty because they were born or because they exist at all. This sense of blame and culpability is a natural feeling for someone who didn't experience bonding with their mother.

Another reason people may deny their separation experience is because of shame and embarrassment. They may think that people will judge them for their mother's rejection. Some people even judge themselves for the negative response of their mother. This shame then turns into denial to protect themselves from such judgment.

Those affected by this should learn as much about the separation as possible. Perhaps they could try talking to their mother or their father. Maybe other family members or friends of the family could shed light on the experience.

Some of these children of NMs may have difficulties dealing with their feelings because they lack emotional support in their lives. They may not manage their emotions correctly because there's no one around to help them through this process. But they must reconcile their past and their feelings as, if left unchecked, it can lead to trouble forming attachments later on in life.

They may also have difficulty expressing their emotions openly toward others because they didn't learn how to do so as a child. They may develop an angry and hostile attitude toward their NM because of this. The loss and deprivation suffered from a separation like this can lead to depression and anxiety in adulthood.

Some of these children have issues with anger management and impulse control. They may act aggressively toward other people, including teachers and classmates. They may feel that their anger stems from their past experiences with an NM as a child.

Working through their emotions with a trusted therapist will allow them to grieve safely for the loss they experienced as children.

They may be afraid to process emotions related to their abuse. Still, they'll be able to do so healthily and productively.

Separated children are often misdiagnosed with other disorders such as attention deficit disorder, depression, anxiety, and even autism. Other conditions can exacerbate the effects of separation, which increases confusion over what disorder is actually at the root of their problems.

The children of NMs may fear that therapy will bring up old wounds and memories best left alone. A therapist will help them work through their worries and healthily process their emotions. The healing process can take many years but is crucial to allow for a fulfilling and satisfying life.

CHAPTER 16

RESETTING YOUR MINDSET: BEYOND TOXIC PARENTING

MANY OF US HAVE COMPLEX post-traumatic stress disorder (CPTSD) brought about by narcissistic parenting. We suffer from extreme trauma, and rates of self-harm and homelessness are incredibly high in today's society. Often, the abuse we experienced in our childhood causes layer upon layer of mental anguish. Our ability to think rationally was taken away from us at a very young age.

It all started with us trusting our primary caregivers, who were supposed to take care of us and keep us safe. They betrayed our trust and turned out to be the very thing that made us the most afraid. They programmed into our unconscious minds what does and doesn't feel safe and what does and doesn't make us happy. We didn't have a choice in the matter. We were made to feel scared, different, and helpless. We took the abuse without ever admitting that what they did was wrong because they were our parents.

These primary caregivers were the worst type of narcissists on this side of the moon. They were the most deceptive people we ever knew. They're the authors of some of the saddest stories we've ever heard. They caused us agony without being able to feel their pain. They forced us to hate ourselves. They made us feel like a failure when we were just defending ourselves against their mental abuse. This is what it's like to face narcissism.

In this chapter, you'll discover how your life doesn't have to be ruined by your NM experiences. You can gain a new perspective on life after your ordeal by acquiring a new perspective, and you'll be able to start afresh.

Key Benefits of a Positive Mindset

Although you may struggle at first, setting yourself the goal of maintaining a positive attitude about yourself and your life will put you on the road to healing from your past trauma.

- You won't need anyone's approval, least of all from a narcissist parent.
- You'll be able to receive positive compliments better.
- You won't need to be in a toxic relationship to feel love.
- You can have a sense of empathy toward others.
- You can detach yourself from toxic people vs. being their hostage.
- You'll never lose yourself in the process.
- You'll do your best to respect yourself.
- You'll retain your sense of morality vs. feeling like a puppet.
- You'll feel more alive.

- You'll improve your productivity at school or work.
- You'll generate more ideas in less time.
- You'll improve your ability to "read" people.
- You'll have better social skills.
- You'll become more confident in yourself.
- You'll be more relaxed and at peace.
- You'll be less defensive and more accepting.
- You'll be able to deal with stress more effectively.
- You'll like yourself, knowing you're doing your best.

The constant emotional demand the narcissist places on their victim is one of the most effective forms of abuse as it works like a trap. Although it takes time to enact, the victim will eventually find themselves in a never-ending cycle of pain, catharsis, and reprieve they feel they can't get out of. Constant emotional demand employs the most draining tactic used in a narcissist's weaponry: a never-ending game of push-and-pull. It's incessant, and the victim's mind tries desperately to ignore the constant requests placed on it by the narcissist, but to no avail. It's like listening to a radio at full volume without being able to switch it off.

It's hard to function when you feel like a silent killer is lurking around every corner. Constant emotional demand is completely draining. Every move you make is accompanied by a voice inside your head telling you that you're not good enough. You're not worthy. You need to do better. When you do or say something that doesn't please the abuser, you're told that you're a waste of space and useless, that you should have done better. Constant emotional demand is a vicious cycle. Once you let it in, it becomes tough to let go, and there might be no way out. When it becomes too much, and it does, it's time to normalize. Take a moment and just breathe. It's time to remind yourself that you're not a waste of space, that you're not useless. You're enough. You don't need to do anything other than concentrate on breathing slowly in and out.

Just think about what it's like to be told that you're a waste of space every day. Often, victims of this type of abuse become accustomed to these destructive statements; they come to believe them and internalize them. This acceptance is a sign of codependency and mind control—the abuser has achieved their goal. But these words *are* incredibly damaging. Day in, day out, it's a never-ending cycle of dull pain. No one should be made to feel worthless. No one should have to endure the constant voice telling them they're hopeless and insignificant. But it's hard to break free from abuse, even when you know that you deserve better than the emotional torture being inflicted on you.

When the victim can leave their abuser and are on their own, they might think, "Finally, I can be me and not have to deal with their constant emotional demands. I can live my life and not have to explain everything that I'm doing. I don't need anybody but myself."

They'll attempt to form new relationships and friendships. They may be successful at first and form bonds with others with ease. However, the abuse, over the long run, has its effects. The survivors of abuse will likely find it hard to build and maintain healthy relationships. Eventually, they might start to pull away from their new support network. They might withdraw and drift, unable to trust others or themselves.

Now, the survivor hears that old voice in their head again, "You're a waste of space."

They need to remember that it's natural to feel like a waste of space, to feel like a failure. But abuse survivors need to remind themselves *why* they think this way. It's not an objective viewpoint. It's the voice of their abuser, who had a specific agenda: to control them.

The survivor can stop these intrusive thoughts and feelings by actively pushing them away and convincing themselves of their worth. But it won't matter unless they confront their notion of what "normal" behavior in a relationship is. Their abuser wasn't treating them with the respect and unconditional love that they merited. They need to clarify that they deserve better and continue to remind themselves that they warrant more from life. A survivor needs to remember that "normal" means a healthy relationship where neither person is thought to be a waste of space. Each person is respected as an independent, strong, and unique being.

As soon as you accept that the abuser's voice is worth less than your own, you'll finally be letting go of the abuse. At last, you'll be gaining a new perspective. And from that new perspective, you might feel a sense of relief, a kind that you've never felt before.

Positive Thinking Leads to Success

The key to getting the most out of life and being happy is considering the implications of your decisions and opting for the ones likely to give you the most favorable outcome.

If you're about to make a decision, consider both the positive and negative outcomes of making that choice and then decide what's best for you. Look at the long term, not just immediate gratification. When you look at the bigger picture, you'll start to make more positive choices. In turn, positive outcomes will help you maintain a positive outlook on life.

When you're faced with challenges, try to stay positive by remembering that you can get through anything. Take into account that things that seem awful now will eventually improve.

Imagine that you're about to run a race with many hurdles for you to jump over to reach the finishing line. Visualize all of the obstacles standing in your way. Though it might seem like a lot, you know that by preparing and pacing yourself, you'll be able to clear them. With positive thinking, a clear head, and sound reasoning, you'll find yourself making it through to the end even if you knock a few hurdles over along the way.

Imagine what it would be like to cross that line and to win. If you win, you'll have to come up with the next strategy to beat your rivals. And eventually, your competition will get tired, give up, or concede defeat.

Remember:

- No matter what happens, try to stay positive.
- Staying positive will make life easier.
- Staying positive will give you a positive future.
- Staying positive will make you happy.
- Staying positive will make you hopeful.
- It's not always easy to stay positive, but most people can do it.

You have to try it. You have to convince yourself that you can. You have to persuade yourself that you'll make your life better.

Positive Thinking Leads to Happiness

A content person experiences life's ups and downs with the attitude that the ebb and flow of happiness are inevitable. They're able to retain a sense of positivity and perspective even when life is complicated as they know that things will always get better. An unhappy person, on the other hand, chalks their unhappiness up to bad luck or fate. They get more depressed, as they feel that they're destined to feel sad all the time and have no control over the matter.

Let's consider a type of person who doesn't see themselves as particularly happy *or* unhappy. They aren't always cheerful. However, they have a great sense of forgiveness, patience, contentment, self-control, and acceptance of themselves and others around them. So, if they find themselves in a terrible situation, they have a better way of dealing with it. Instead of "wishing they were dead" or being in denial, they recognize the problem for what it is and then deal with it however best they can.

What does this type of person do that so many others don't? They see the big picture. They consider all the factors and how best to react to them. And finally, instead of letting their state of affairs get the better of them, they calmly and acceptingly deal with it. The result? They're happy with how things turn out for them, as they feel in control and are prepared to deal with whatever's thrown their way.

To feel happy, you need to feel good about yourself. It means accepting yourself for your better qualities *and* your flaws. It means acknowledging that life isn't always going to be easy. And it's about realizing that people are never going to be perfect. When people are happy with themselves, they're more likely to overcome any problems they face. They're less likely to become depressed or have suicidal thoughts. We must make time for self-care and self-love.

There are many ways to improve your levels of happiness instantly, too. In today's world, we're all working hard during the day and then immersing ourselves in social media at night. It's essential to take the time out to do things that bring us genuine joy.

Discover new hobbies, or return to activities that you used to enjoy as a child. Don't worry about what other people will think. If you want to take up finger painting again, go for it! These activities could be done in a group or on your own; as long as you're having fun, that's what counts.

Socializing is a great way to improve your mood. Meet up with friends or join societies or groups to meet new people who share the same interests as you. Talking to other people and feeling that you're being listened to is a sure-fire way to make you feel happy and content.

Whether you live in an urban or rural area, go outside. Going for even a short walk will lift your spirits as you get the blood pumping through your veins. If you're able to, reconnect with nature by taking the time to look around you and admire the different trees, plants, and wildlife you see on your way.

There are so many ways you can rediscover your spark, your happiness. Remember that when you're happy, you can become anything you desire.

Become Well Adjusted and Calm

Sometimes, we'll wake up in a bad mood for no good reason. If we don't shake it off by the time we've had breakfast, it'll probably ruin the rest of our day. It's hard to get a perspective on things when you feel grumpy, angry, tired, or miserable.

When you have a bad day, week, or month, it can feel never-ending. But you must remember that whenever you feel overwhelmed, resentful, or helpless, these feelings are only temporary. Even our darkest moments will eventually end.

You always have to take a step back and look at the situation from a different perspective to see the big picture. Trust that things get better over time.

Taking a step back doesn't mean that you don't deal with the issues you're facing. Taking a step back doesn't mean that you succumb to the problems that have been thrown your way. What it means is that you reduce the intensity of your situation every time you deal with it. You let go of the emotional baggage and feel prepared to face the next challenge that comes your way.

The next time you have a bad day, week, or month, just take a step back. Take a deep breath, roll up your sleeves, and face your problems with perspective and determination.

Strategies to Reset Your Mindset and Feel Better

Trying to be positive will do you wonders, whether this means focusing on the good in any given situation, turning a disadvantage into a benefit, or telling yourself that things will improve. By putting yourself in a positive mindset, you'll be able to face problems head-on.

Sometimes you'll need to get emotional support. Talk to someone whom you trust and who'll listen to you without judgment. Often, people feel better when they cry and vent, releasing their emotions instead of bottling them up. Don't be afraid of letting it all out.

Don't forget the importance of socializing. No man is an island. Spending time with other people will help you put your problems in perspective, allow you to share your best qualities, and help you feel wanted and needed. Take time to do things with other people that make you laugh, as this will make life seem less dark and lonely.

To reset your mind, you can use visualization to create a little fantasy world for yourself. Imagine an ideal scenario for yourself and think about how you can achieve it. By setting goals, you can focus your energy and creativity on something positive.

Meditation and relaxation are excellent ways to release tension, help you sleep at night, and re-set your energy levels. The mind is powerful, and you need to train it to work for you rather than against you.

Remember that it's essential to love yourself, flaws and all. Keep in mind that everybody makes mistakes, and these can only make us stronger. Forgive yourself, learn from it, and move on. Accepting yourself will help you to be more compassionate and will enable the formation of strong bonds and relationships.

It's important to remember that it's okay to feel vulnerable and alone sometimes. There's a chance that you'll get hurt again. But by taking responsibility for yourself, your thoughts, and your actions, you'll put yourself on the path to controlling your own destiny. You deserve a good life filled with love, appreciation, and hope.

Remember that it's never too late for anything—you can still follow your dreams! Make sure that you're living your life according to your own wants and needs. Don't let the voice of your abuser get in the way of you achieving this.

You're reading this book because you've chosen to get better, the choice to become happier. Hopefully, we've started to show you how this can be done. It's up to you to take what you learn, imagine how different a life you can have, and take action. You're now in control.

A Word on Narcissistic Abuse and Stockholm Syndrome

Contrary to popular belief, narcissists hate themselves. This self-loathing is why they try to make everybody else as miserable as they are. They're liars, manipulators, and charlatans presenting themselves as gurus, mentors, and leaders. Their victims are traumatized by the constant abuse, be it mental, emotional, or physical.

Some narcissists' victims develop Stockholm syndrome as a psychological response to their abuse. Stockholm syndrome involves identifying and bonding with the abuser and cooperating with them.

If you suffer from Stockholm syndrome, you'll believe that your abuser is right, that they love you, and that they need you. You'll feel compelled to protect your abuser, even from the police, and that the two of you are a team, a couple, a cooperating duo. Stockholm syndrome involves a hostage-like effect and a trauma bond, making it difficult for the abused to escape.

One of the strategies that can help you overcome Stockholm syndrome is to "zoom out" of your experience—to take a mental step away from your situation. Doing so will enable you to realize how detached you are from your experience. It can help you understand what your abuser is really doing to you and how they're using you for personal gain.

To enable yourself to overcome Stockholm syndrome, you'll need to realize that the abuser mistreats you not because they love you but because they have a disturbing agenda. If they loved you, they would respect you, and their treatment of you says otherwise.

You'll need to realize that it's not too late for you. You don't have to fear your abuser. Recognize that your abuser is mentally unstable and needs professional help. There's nothing that you can do for them. Understand that they're harming you, and you need to leave. You need to know that your abuser isn't the boss of you, and only you should have the power to be in control of yourself.

Choosing to be free from your abuser will do you a huge favor. Freedom will make your life easier and happier. Liberation will make you a better person, more confident, honest with yourself, and someone you can be proud of. Escaping the narcissist's clutches will create positivity and enjoyment in your life.

CHAPTER 17

THE ART OF MEDITATION

NARCISSISTIC ABUSE IS CONSIDERED one of the worst kinds of abuse because it damages the victim's mind and spirit. The victim becomes a "slave" to the narcissist, living their life to please or rescue their abuser.

In this section, a survivor of narcissistic abuse tells her story. She describes how through meditation, psychotherapy, and her strong will to understand herself, she found the way out of her abusive situation and healed herself. She then went on to start the healing journey of others with a therapy that she created. Her story reveals what happens to a narcissistic abuse victim's mind and spirit and how the abuser and victims are ruled by an insecure, obsessed, distorted sense of self.

Narcissism itself is considered to be a form of addiction and a psychological disorder by therapists. This survivor's story has been thoughtfully written and laid out to heal both victims and survivors of narcissistic abuse and narcissistic parents to help with their mental health.

Narcissistic abuse is a complex word that most people and professionals in mental health haven't understood yet. The main reason for this is that the victims or survivors of this abuse are made to feel so guilty for bringing it up, and this guilt has not allowed the victims to receive proper help or treatment. There are hardly any support groups for the survivors and almost no therapists who understand narcissistic abuse. Victims are often set up in therapy to fight and argue with their abusers, which isn't what the victim wants. The victim just wants to heal and understand.

The main reason that healing this type of abuse is hard is the low self-esteem and negative self-image that most of these victims have. The brain structure of a victim causes them to believe they're the problem, and this is why until this is realized, they can't heal. This is the most crucial factor in healing. There are many narcissists in this world. Most of them are undetected and living their lives while using and exploiting other people. This isn't good for anyone's mental health. Many narcissists have killed their lovers, spouses, and people who got in their way. The interesting thing about narcissists is that they're often very charismatic people who get away with their behavior until they're caught. If one isn't careful, a narcissist can even use them to get away with a crime.

Extracting themselves from the abusive situation is also a big challenge for the victims. Like me, those who are married or have children with a narcissist usually have a much harder time, especially if the narcissist has custody. This can also get very expensive and put a financial burden on the victim, which can also cause them to become emotionally bankrupt and exhausted.

Narcissists drain all of their victims in varying degrees and cause them to lose all self-esteem.

Therapy is available for those who are willing to find it. Professional training in narcissistic abuse for psychotherapists and mental health professionals will help them understand this type of abuse and develop methods to guide survivors' healing processes.

I managed to escape my narcissist after several attempts. When I was eventually free, I didn't realize the immense work that was ahead of me. Luckily, I was recommended a therapist who specialized in helping victims of domestic and narcissistic abuse. She helped to start the process of piecing back together my life, my sense of self, and my self-worth.

It wasn't easy. Sometimes the pain of confronting my abuse felt more traumatic than when it had happened at the time. But I stood firm. I didn't want my abuser to have his power over me still. I didn't want him to win. And I wanted to fight for my children, for them to see that their mom is strong and in control.

My therapist suggested that I find additional ways to cope with the trauma I'd experienced and its effects. I discovered meditation through the community center, where my kids had their dance lessons. I can honestly say that it's one habit that has made an incredible, positive impact on my mental health. Meditation is a powerful tool, not just in healing from narcissistic abuse but in handling stressful situations throughout life.

Meditation soothes your mind. It helps you clear out your negative emotions and heal them on a subconscious level. The great thing is, you don't have to pay money or leave the house to do it. There are so many books, audiobooks, YouTube videos, and podcasts that can guide you through the process.

The key to meditating is focusing on your breathing. I'll describe a simple technique that I use every day:

Make sure that you're sitting or lying down in a comfortable position. Breathe in through your nose for four seconds and hold it in for four seconds. Exhale for four seconds, and hold the empty breath for four seconds.

When you first try this technique, doing it for just ten minutes a day will make a difference. You can then build up to practicing it for up to 20 minutes a day.

Remember to focus on your breathing. The idea is to breathe in, calming your body, and breathe out, releasing any tension. Imagine your body is in a state of neutrality. At first, you may notice your breathing is rapid and shallow. This is what happens when we're anxious and nervous. Bring your focus back to your breath and try to breathe through your nose. Listen to your breath, and notice how slow it is when you calm down. The goal of meditation is to reach that level of slow, deep breathing.

You'll find that this process clears out old emotions, feelings, and any addictions that weaken you. I do it daily, sometimes twice. You can do it when you start to feel anxious or as a great way to go into the day feeling refreshed and optimistic. Sometimes it works well for me at night when I'm finding it difficult to get to sleep.

Meditation is soothing, uplifting, and relaxing. It helps you feel centered and in control. As you meditate, you'll free yourself from the effects of stress, anxiety, and depression.

Another great technique that helps alleviate self-criticism and self-hatred and leads to true self-compassion is loving-kindness meditation. It's very gentle without any religious or spiritual connotations, making it accessible to anyone. To put it simply, all you do is silently repeat uplifting phrases.

You can't make up your mind to love yourself in just a few days. It's a long-term practice. But with loving-kindness meditation, you can make a start by bringing to your mind several memories linked to happiness, contentment, and love. This type of meditation will help to develop positive feelings about yourself, eventually leading to a more compassionate and connected relationship with yourself and with others.

Here's how I practice loving-kindness meditation:

1. Repeat the following phrases, silently or out loud, for a few minutes. Feel the sensations in your body; let the warmth, love, and acceptance penetrate you.

You're okay, just as you are.

May I forgive myself for my mistakes.

May I be at peace with myself.

May I know I am loveable just as I am.

2. *Then repeat the following phrases for a few minutes. Let the emotion of love permeate your being. Try to feel the warmth and love from your heart.*

May I be safe.

May I be healthy.

May I be happy.

May I be peaceful and at ease.

3. *Repeat these following phrases to wish happiness and peace for others.*

May all people be safe.

May all people be healthy.

May all people be happy.

May all people be peaceful and at ease.

May all people know they are loveable.

Meditative healing can be done anywhere, anytime, and you don't need to set aside a sacred space in which to practice it. You can do it with your eyes open or closed. You can choose any phrases that feel right for you, but you can use the ones above to begin with. If you're conscious of the changes occurring within you, you'll see that your narcissistic abuse recovery has already started. Keep practicing the loving-kindness meditation as often as you can. The more you practice meditation, the greater the benefits for your mind, body, and soul.

I just want to end by saying that any victim or survivor of abuse should never give up hope. There's always a way out of your torture. I know that long after you've physically distanced yourself from your abuser that the mental and emotional chains can still weigh heavy. But you owe it to yourself to get help, whether that's from a professional, friends, or other family members. You need to practice self-love and find healthy ways to help you on your journey to healing and acceptance. I wish you all the best and hope that my story has helped you in some way.

CHAPTER 18

HOW TO START HEALING FROM NARCISSISTIC PARENTING

SOLUTION ONE: Leave the Emotionally-Abusive Relationship

The first step in recovering from narcissistic abuse, toxic parents, and complex post-traumatic stress disorder (CPTSD) is to leave the narcissist. This may sound simple, but it's not easy to let a parent go. Distancing ourselves from a parent plays into our deep-rooted sense of feeling rejected, deserted, and unloved. We may think that we're breaking an unspoken promise never to leave our abuser. But we have to realize that we don't owe our abuser anything. It's not up to us to rescue them. They broke their promise to us to keep us safe and out of harm's way.

But we have to want our freedom. We're the ones who have to decide what we're going to do. We have to decide to stop waiting for them to save us. Only we can set the borders and boundaries that'll help us prevent the abuse. By making these choices and taking action, we'll open ourselves up to "embracing" our pain, and this is how we stop being the victim.

We have to decide to stop beating ourselves up. We need to sit down and work through why we gave unconditional love to our abusers for so long. We have to call out all the lies they told us that we believed. We have to distance ourselves from everyone who enables them. We have to focus on ourselves for once.

Solution Two: Cut Off All Contact With Your Abuser(s)

Emotionally manipulative relationships are sources of our trauma, and unless we leave them, they'll continue to harm and scar us. Despite all the promises they made to us, our narcissistic parents never had our back. They weren't our friends or saviors. We have to realize that they don't hold power over us anymore.

We have to start seeing things as they truly are, and only distance from our abusers will allow this to happen. This is the only way we'll find long-lasting happiness. We're the ones slowly poisoning ourselves by staying in toxic relationships. We're the ones who'll end up destroying our sanity. There's no point trying to hold on to false hope while the truth is staring us in the face.

We can't pretend that we don't feel the pain of the people closest to us. After all, we're human. We're programmed to care, to nurture, to love, to empathize. But we have to be careful. We can't let emotion rule our heads. We need to be rational and sensible and make decisions that we won't regret for the rest of our lives. We need to do what we've been putting off for a long time: stop all contact with our abuser. This step is how we start to take care of ourselves, make sense of our experience, and start getting our lives back.

Solution Three: Face the People Causing the Problems

We can't change what happened to us in the past. However, we can prevent it from happening again by stopping behaviors in the present. We must learn to deal with the people who are still creating problems for us today. We didn't choose the family we were born into, but we can choose to detach ourselves from them and the chaos that they create.

Detaching ourselves doesn't have to mean that we can't maintain relationships with them. It just means that we shouldn't depend on them. It means that we need to learn to be happy without them. We must discover how to care about ourselves for once. We must stop allowing them the power to create chaos in our life. We must learn to trust ourselves. When we start to take control, we can make decisions based on our values rather than the narcissist's projections.

Solution Four: Stop the Self-Torture

It's up to us to set our boundaries, quit playing their games, and stop allowing them to dictate who we are. The control they have over our lives has to end. We have to stop making ourselves dependent on them. They're not our source of happiness or security. By taking back control, we'll be able to bring back our sanity.

And we have to stop the self-torture. Victims of abuse feel guilty for "letting" the abuse happen. Realize that you weren't to blame. We have to stop thinking that there's a way that we can "fix" our parents. Remember that we're only in control of ourselves. We torture ourselves by thinking that we should try to understand our parents, but this is wrong. We should stop feeling attached to people who don't love us. We have to stop running from our feelings of hurt and pain and confront them head-on. We have to stop torturing ourselves that we're not good enough. We need to stop, stop, stop.

We don't need toxic parents in our lives. We weren't brought into this world for them to use and abuse. We're moving on and reclaiming our lives. We can get out of the cycle of toxic relationships and emotional abuse and become truly happy.

Solution Five: Take Back Your Power in Relationships and Respect Yourself

We're emotional survivors of an emotional terrorist and aren't looking for any more pain in our lives. We need to break the cycle of abuse by not allowing ourselves to get into a situation that could create more pain or suffering. The painful reality is that our family of origin exploited us. They took our life away. They used us for their purpose. They hurt us. Realizing this makes the process of emotional recovery difficult and can make us question whether or not it's possible to recover.

In retrospect, we see that our toxic parents created the environment, circumstances, and conditions to get what they wanted. They destroyed us. They left us alone and isolated, made us dependent, gave us false hope, and pretended to love us. They never let us know that we need to find happiness or could find happiness without them. They never let us know that we could live and survive without them.

Taking control and learning how to respect yourself is a vital step in the process of emotional recovery. We must learn to walk away from people and situations that cause emotional pain. We must discover how to be independent and how to take care of ourselves. We must feel comfortable with solitude and without the love of others. We must find joy in our own life, doing things by ourselves. We must find our happiness, learning for ourselves, and taking care of ourselves. Overall, we must learn to love ourselves.

All of this will be hard for us because we aren't used to doing this. We never had any responsibility for our life before. We didn't know that this was something that we need to do as all decisions were made for us. Other people shaped our whole self-identity and self-worth. But taking control is the only way for us to heal and get better. We'll enable ourselves to let go of the pain from our past.

Solution Six: Heal Your Childhood Wounds

There are many reasons you may feel you've struggled your whole life with diminishing self-esteem and no sense of your "rightful" place in the world. Living day in and day out with a narcissist will smash your sense of worth and identity. There are many resources for healing and finding increased self-worth available to you. These resources can provide you with the tools and direction to change your future.

Enjoy your new well-being and the healing you're experiencing, having now escaped your toxic parents. Focus all your attention on the fact that you're free to be your person. You're not a child anymore. You're not a victim anymore. You are, finally, *you*.

You won't be able to enjoy your freedom if you can't admit that you were abused in the first place. It isn't your fault that your parents chose to manipulate you. You're an adult now, and you can decide to live your life free of the burden they inflicted on you. You can start living your own life and making your own choices today.

The choices are now yours to make. You can choose to forgive them or not. You can decide to have them in your life or not. There's no right or wrong decision, as long as it's coming from you and only you.

You can choose to feel ill as often as you feel well. You can choose for your emotions to overwhelm you at times. You can decide if you're going to feel sad, angry, or indifferent. You have a choice. You're not a product of your parents' abuse. You are your own person—not a victim, but a *survivor*.

It's now up to you to take your future into your own hands. You can choose to stop hurting yourself and start to do whatever you need to do to feel good. Now is the time to put your own needs first.

CHAPTER 19

HOW TO HEAL FROM COMPLEX POST-TRAUMATIC STRESS DISORDER (CPTSD) CAUSED BY A NARCISSISTIC PARENT

YOU MAY NOT FEEL STRONG, but you are. You're resilient and have the power to control where you go from here. Victims of trauma have to remind themselves of their capacity to heal. Recovery is a personal process; it may take months, or it may take years. But you can do it. It may be tough, but the rewards will outweigh the struggle.

Victims of abuse will often develop mechanisms to help them cope with their trauma. They may be in denial of their pain or the abuse that they've suffered. They may have become used to feeling hurt, angry, sad, or worthless. Sometimes they become like their abuser, lacking in emotional empathy or compassion.

People who've suffered abuse may have a false sense of self-awareness. They're in distress but can't recognize it or address it.

They don't know how to process and manage their emotions and feelings.

You might never believe you're worth the justice you deserve, but you need to accept that you won't be whole until you've addressed your past and realize that you're worthy of a second chance at life.

You likely have complex post-traumatic stress disorder (CPTSD) caused by narcissistic abuse. Complex trauma occurs when a person is exposed to prolonged and repetitive emotional trauma, most typically in childhood. People who experience complex trauma commonly develop high levels of susceptibility to stress, often exhibiting emotionally unintegrated responses to ordinary stressors. It'll take time and work to get better, but you can do it.

You need to find a therapist, someone who understands what has to be done to help you heal. You'd benefit from establishing a relationship with a therapist who understands that abuse causes trauma, leading to anxiety and depression. A good therapist will know that you're fighting with your brain and can help you work through that. The best therapist is one who knows that you're trying to reconcile your past and present. You need a professional who'll listen to you and believe in you.

Remember that you deserve to be in a loving relationship. You deserve to be independently wealthy. You deserve happiness and peace.

HEALING FROM EMOTIONAL FLASHBACKS

It's a struggle to heal our psyche and minds if we've grown up with narcissistic parents. The emotional wounds the abuse leaves behind can appear in the form of emotional flashbacks. These are incidents where an event or word triggers us, and we vividly experience an original upset or trauma from childhood. Often, the feelings, body sensations, and/or visualizations are experienced as though they're real or life-threatening.

Our reality becomes distorted, causing us to feel confused and disorientated. We tend to misunderstand why these flashbacks are happening to us or deny that they're connected to our past trauma.

One of the best ways to resolve these painful memories and emotions is to process them by writing them down. This way, the emotional flashback can be fixed, allowing the past's emotional effects to subside and the more permanent changes to be assimilated and integrated.

Journaling is a therapeutic writing exercise where you can free yourself from your emotional past. Journaling is a powerful tool used in all aspects of recovery from narcissistic abuse. Writing is a natural, physical human response and has the tremendous ability to achieve healing. The healing extends to the mind, body, heart, and soul. Journaling is a process of self-love, self-nurturing, being the observer of oneself, and self-discovery. This therapeutic act supports and enhances the integrated self and healthy relationships.

Through journaling, we can become balanced and grounded. The spiritual dimension of journaling is the tool of transforming the structure of the human mind and spirit. The practice of journaling helps one learn to be self-reflective and self-aware. For many, writing is one of the most powerful ways to access their true self, heal, and reintegrate fragmented parts of the mind.

Writing down your thoughts, feelings, and emotions is one of the best ways to develop self-awareness. Being self-aware is essential to be free. The self-reflection that comes through journaling is necessary for personal growth and spiritual connection. The importance of emotional mirroring, validation, nurturing, and love becomes all the clearer. Self-reflection and journaling help us learn to be less needful and avoidant. Journaling is a process of coming to terms with things, becoming clearer about what we want, and creating personal meaning.

It's also helpful to write down your goals — what do you want from your new life? These can be big ambitions, such as getting a college degree, or small aims, such as reading the latest best-seller. By writing these down, you won't lose track of your dreams, and you'll be clear about what direction you want your life to go in.

HEALING FROM TOXIC SHAME

Many survivors of narcissistic abuse find themselves drowning in shame. Shame is an emotional state where you feel disgusting, unworthy, and damaged. It's the belief that you're unlovable, undeserving, undesirable, and defective. You think that your past determines the future and that both lack value or worth.

The causes of feelings of shame are numerous, including traumatization, shame training, dissociation, the "enemy within" mindset, abuse, neglect, socialization, boundaries, abuse, abandonment, and more. It's an experience of constant fear and horror, manifesting itself through a narrowed field of vision and a diminished ability to see oneself, thoughts, and feelings with clarity.

Moral, ethical, and spiritual development all grow from a shame-free heart. Developing these qualities is essential for gaining freedom, self-worth, joy, intimacy, and healthy relationships. Taking the time to do daily self-nurturing and self-love through therapeutic practices will help you integrate this healthy mindset into your daily life.

Many people with NMs have been brought up to feel as though they're "bad." To recover from the shame this abuse has caused, the active cultivation of self-nurturing is required. The children of NMs must remember that their mothers were flawed individuals—not them. Practicing self-nurturing may cause one to realize just how valuable and strong they are.

Many who have NMs are also survivors of dissociation. The experience of dissociation is centered on a dominant fear of being emotionally vulnerable. Because of this emotional vulnerability, the victim tries to run away from the pain the abuse has caused. In other words, they dissociate to avoid it. This disconnection is dangerous. It's equivalent to putting a bandage on a deep wound without cleaning it out, stitching it up, or changing the dressing over time. The result is that the wound festers and begins to stink.

It may cause other infections or illnesses. To heal, the survivor must gradually strengthen their sense of self-worth and undergo therapy.

Oversharing is the opposite of dissociation. Rather than disconnecting from their shame, victims express themselves too much to relieve their emotional and physical tension. To heal, they must learn about balance. They need to become aware of the negative consequences of their actions on others. They must learn to be mindful of when they're too invasive in conversations, to slow down, and have a sense of alertness when it comes to speaking. They need to learn to respect their own and others' boundaries.

A narcissistic-based relationship is one where one person is overly controlling, manipulative, and domineering. The person who's in control is the ringleader. They're the person who dictates the rules within a relationship and enforces them. Their victim is bullied into submission, put down, and denied their ambitions or desires.

Every person's life is about relationships with others. It's through relationships with others that we experience joy, pain, sorrow, and love. It's also through relationships with others that people form their identities. To be complete, people need to know who they are without others. They need to know who they are without reliance on others.

The problem with narcissistic relationships is that they're abusive. They're designed to make the person who's controlled suffer. The person they control evolves into an enabler, enabling their abuser to treat them as they wish and without boundaries.

You can step away from the toxic shame created by narcissistic relationships by surrounding yourself with the support you need to heal. Walk away from people who disrespect, demean, and abuse you. You're worth the best in life. You're worth the genuine love and care of others.

HEALING FROM SELF-ABANDONMENT

The children of narcissistic parents will often have an "enemy within." Their parents put them down. They felt worthless and unlovable. They were frequently left helpless when they showed any sort of emotion not sanctioned by their parents. As a result, they believe that they can't feel or express their feelings. They think that they should hide their thoughts and emotions, developing a "split self." Although they're attached to their physical form, they feel numb to their bodies and emotions. This type of dissociation from the body and the self is called self-abandonment.

A person with narcissistic parents will feel disconnected from themselves and may feel that they shouldn't have the thoughts and feelings that they do. To help with the self-abandonment, they should keep a daily journal. This daily writing will reduce anxiety and dissociation by making them aware of their thoughts and emotions. The journal keeps their thoughts and feelings real and alive. Journaling will allow the survivor to move towards a healthier sense of self and more beneficial relationships with others. They'll heal through gaining more self-nurturing skills, dealing productively with their issues, and feeling better about themselves. They'll learn how to gain back control of their lives.

Through this process, they learn to heal their emotional wounds, erase their split personality, and rehabilitate themselves.

The more they write, the more the survivor will know themselves. The more they know themselves, the less they'll be in danger. Writing will help them for the rest of their life. This practice is about educating oneself about life. It's about creating a sense of self-mastery and control.

Journaling will help survivors understand why they were harmed. It'll make them realize that they weren't crazy or to blame for what happened to them, that they were abused and that the narcissist will always blame someone else for anything that goes wrong. The journal helps the survivor realize that the narcissist was a sick individual who used them for personal gain.

Journaling is a safe way for a person to digest their pain and clear their mind of the mental anguish plaguing them. A journal is a place where a person can control their pain and start to get healthy again. Writing is a safe practice; it can't harm the writer or judge them. A journal is a place where a person can feel calmer in the face of their pain.

This practice is about respecting how it feels to have pain and how it feels to have been harmed. It feels good to be healthy. It feels good to feel better about yourself. A journal is a tool for uncovering what was happening behind the scenes, learning from that experience, and moving on.

Journaling doesn't need to be done in secret. It's up to the individual if they want to show it to anybody or not. It may be a good idea to have a trusted mentor read it with them for extra support and encouragement. Sharing the pain of abuse can lift its burden. The journal will be part of their life for as long as they think that it's useful.

HEALING FROM YOUR INNER CRITIC

The "voice" inside the head of an abuse victim is often cruel, mean, nasty, and self-destructive. The victim has been taught to see the world through the eyes of their abuser. This voice, or inner critic, isn't rational, reasonable, or objective. It's not based on reality. Knowing how to heal from your inner critic is a valuable step in your recovery. You'll be able to overcome the horrible psychological, emotional, physical, mental, or sexual abuse that you've endured by turning your inner voice to your advantage.

You and your inner voice are the same entity. When you hear your inner critic speak, it's you talking to yourself. For many people, their inner voice can be a force for good. It helps keep them on the straight and narrow, analyze situations rationally, and even calms them down when they're feeling stressed. The abuse victim's inner voice is a vicious, mean critic that's been placed on their psyche through years of trauma and abuse. This voice must be re-programmed so that they can live freely without feeling self-doubt or unworthiness.

The more you know about this inner critic, the better you'll deal with it and overcome it. You must harness the power of your inner voice healthily and productively. If not, it can make you bitter, ignorant, powerless, and unable to succeed in life.

You can get rid of it by simply *not listening* to it. Don't take any notice of a single word it's telling you. The reason your inner critic spoke to you wasn't because of some self-reflection or self-evaluation. It wasn't placed in your mind to help you improve. It's purely there to control you, to lock you into a life that you didn't choose. Because of this voice, you've lost your ability to make any conscious decisions. You're a puppet of this inner critic. It always makes you feel bad about yourself and increases your sense of helplessness.

We're not talking about you finally being able to forgive the voice. You need to *eradicate* it. You have to put an end to the abuse.

This process will entail some serious mind-over-matter. You're going to have to completely block off the internal noise until it's not there anymore. Stop listening to it and tell yourself that you're not the one doing anything wrong. Only then will you be completely free of negative programming.

Yes, this is all easier said than done. It'll take all your effort, attention, and perseverance to block out your inner critic. You have to keep telling yourself that you're worthy of a happy life, that you're not to blame for your past, and that you're doing the very best you can. It's up to you to free yourself of the untold amount of negative programming that's been with you since birth.

You can't beat addiction by merely putting down the substance that fueled it. It goes deeper than that. It takes time and self-reflection. You'll need to unpack your past while telling yourself that you're worth the effort. And be careful—your inner critic will always be the first thing that rears its ugly head when you're feeling at your most vulnerable. You'll have to recognize it for what it is and kick it straight to the curb.

CHAPTER 20

STOP LABELING YOURSELF AS A VICTIM: SEVEN WAYS TO HEAL

FROM CHILDHOOD, we're given the impression that being a victim means being alone, isolated, and invisible. People who've suffered from abuse may find it hard to shake the label of "victim." Sometimes, defining or describing themselves as a "victim" becomes their way of coping with trauma and pain and distancing themselves from the rest of the world.

But we need to define ourselves by more than just our past abuse. We're human beings who deserve to be seen, loved, accepted and respected. To heal and recover, we need to identify the unique characteristics that make us individuals in our own right.

Here are seven ways to STOP labeling yourself as a victim and start living an empowered life.

1. Understand how your perspective influences you.

Our hardwiring is the blueprint for our lives. Our perspective is the lens through which we view it, and our life experiences reinforce that perspective. Our genetic endowments combine with our life experiences to form the core of who we are. Your hardwiring is a combination of all of your genes plus your life experiences. Certain things in your life will set off the "trauma alarm" and bring about a flashback to repressed memories. This results in PTSD.

Some people go their whole lives never understanding why they feel out of control, have anxiety, are depressed, or have panic attacks. Understanding that our feelings are an acute or chronic response to past trauma helps us see why we live the way we do and know the best way to deal with our thoughts and emotions.

Sometimes we're too caught up in "should" and "should not" to realize that the way we're viewing the world is creating our life story. We carry certain beliefs, fears, and self-talk into every situation. Often, we're unaware of them or how much a role they play in our lives and experiences.

We can't break free of the victim-label until we stop looking at the world through it.

2. Free yourself from guilt.

The boundaries between guilt, shame, and fear are often so intertwined and complicated that a victim-label can feel like a get-out-of-jail-free card. We can use it as a way to not face up to our problems and an excuse not to face our abuse.

But guilt is a nasty, manipulative feeling that only serves to keep us trapped in the victim role. In recovery, we learn to free ourselves from guilt and therefore rid ourselves of the label of "victim."

3. Love yourself.

People who identify as victims tend to see themselves as "not worthy." They push others away because they feel unworthy of love, attention, or respect. An "unworthy" person doesn't even know what to do with love, as they've never experienced it before, even if it's freely given to them.

While this may be off-putting to most people, many people with predatory or manipulative tendencies find this trait very appealing. The "dark side" of their personality seeks out vulnerable people, and you'll run the risk of falling prey to further abuse.

You must learn to love yourself again, respect yourself, and trust your instincts. In this way, you'll toss aside the victim-label and keep yourself safe from people with bad intentions.

4. Reject your victim-identity.

Most victims were manipulated in some way. They would have had a hard time saying no to their abuser and then beat themselves up about it later.

To reject the label of "victim," you'll have to be willing to get uncomfortable. When we're ready to face our pain, we'll be able to develop a new pattern of behavior. First, you'll need to learn how to fake it.

- Fake feeling okay.
- Fake feeling calm, happy, and relaxed before, during, and after your interactions.
- Fake being in control of your emotions.
- Fake being okay with not getting what you want.
- Fake it until you make it.

For a long time now, you may have just settled for the crumbs that life threw at you. As a victim, you were probably conditioned to think that was all you deserved. When you get comfortable with being uncomfortable, you start to believe that you can contribute something to the world and are justified in getting the life you want. You'll feel that you deserve to be treated with respect.

5. Develop boundaries.

The first step to gaining boundaries is learning to say no calmly, assertively, efficiently, and confidently. Boundaries are non-negotiable, and they shouldn't be up for discussion.

When you set up these boundaries, remember:

- Don't let anyone make any excuses for not respecting your wishes.
- You don't need to give any explanations.
- Don't allow drama.
- Don't argue.
- Decide what's acceptable to you and stick to it.

When you start putting boundaries in place, you become empowered. The victim-label starts losing some of its influence over your life. You can use limits to begin taking control of your life back from the people around you.

6. Commit to a Self-Love Lifestyle.

When you're putting boundaries in place, it can sometimes hurt other people's feelings. They might not understand what's going on, or they may be in denial about what's happened to you. This can apply both to your abuser and others that you know.

But these boundaries have to be respected by *everyone*. It's the only way you'll claw back your self-respect and self-worth.

So, during this time (and beyond), you need to practice self-love. This practice means setting time aside for yourself, being selfish if you have to, learning methods to heal and relax you, spending time doing what you enjoy. It means shutting out the noise from other people who won't respect your need for time and space on your own.

7. See the gift.

The victim-label comes with a gift. This may sound strange, but it's true. It's up to you to acknowledge it and change your perspective. This gift is your compassion, your empathic tendencies—your ability to feel deeply for yourself and others.

The gift may have developed while you were a victim, but you can now use it to your advantage. Your sensitivity and compassion can help you learn more about yourself. It can even help you assist others who've had similar experiences and motivate and inspire them.

You can use this gift of compassion and empathy in all aspects of your life. Your studies, work, friendships, and relationships will all prosper because of it. You might become an advocate for others who've suffered from abuse. From victim to survivor to champion of others—it's a realistic goal that you can achieve.

CONCLUSION

This book is a superb resource for anyone who's been affected by growing up in a narcissistic family. You've not only learned how to heal from your childhood wounds but how to help others going through the trauma or grief caused by toxic relationships. You'll be able to navigate future relationships by putting your past experiences into perspective, understanding where they came from, and how they affect your present and future.

You'll now be able to begin healing from your past emotional trauma and build healthy relationships with minimal to no emotional manipulation symptoms.

With relief from the symptoms of childhood abuse, you'll begin to feel free from the emotional trauma you've held on to for far too long. With this newfound freedom, you'll be able to create beautiful relationships with others and develop a life for yourself without pain, confusion, or feelings of inadequacy or shame.

This book is a must-have for abused children and anyone who wishes to feel happy and free in their relationships.

You can now stop living as a victim of narcissistic parenting, emotional pain, or the constant trigger of past emotional trauma. Today is the start of a wonderful, fulfilling life.
– Happiness Factory

THANK YOU

THANK YOU FOR PURCHASING THIS BOOK!

The Happiness Factory Book Series is dedicated to helping you resolve the problems you face in your relationships. We have a dedicated team of researchers, writers, and editors who work tirelessly to provide you with the best information to inform and inspire you.

We understand that the issues you may be facing can be extremely stressful. We strive to help you find ways to resolve these so that you can see a bright, hopeful future for yourself.

We offer reliable and accurate information that's useful for both men and women. People of all ages can receive help from this book and use it to enhance their personal lives.

We look forward to reading your comments. These will help us provide an even better experience for you in the future.

Made in the USA
Las Vegas, NV
12 April 2022